SCIENCE 1107
EQUILIBRIUM SYSTEMS

CONTENTS

Author: Harold Wengert, Ed.D.
Editor: Alan Christopherson, M.S.
Illustrations: Alpha Omega Graphics
                  Kyle Bennett, A.S.

Alpha Omega Publications®

804 N. 2nd Ave. E., Rock Rapids, IA 51246-1759
© MM by Alpha Omega Publications, Inc.   All rights reserved.
LIFEPAC is a registered trademark of Alpha Omega Publications, Inc.

EQUILIBRIUM SYSTEMS

Our universe is in a constant state of decay. Since the Fall of man, our universe was locked into the bondage of corruption, which is plainly evident in the physical world.

Equilibrium systems exist throughout nature. You are a walking equilibrium system. When your system is out of equilibrium, you are probably sick. The force of increasing entropy countering the force of decreasing enthalpy is at the heart of our study of equilibrium systems. Thus, after the Fall, the natural balance between these two forces was upset and the balance shifted to the decay, or random motion (entropy), side of the equilibrium. The energy source is running down and is lost to the environment. However, this state will be banished once the great work of redemption has been consummated by Christ, and the "new heavens and new earth" (Isaiah 65:17; 66:22; 2 Peter 3:13; and Revelation 21:1) are established by the power of God.

This LIFEPAC® will help you to understand some of the common equilibriums around us, what affects their state, and how they can be altered. Much of what you have already learned will be applied in this LIFEPAC.

OBJECTIVES

Read these objectives. The objectives tell you what you will be able to do when you have successfully completed this LIFEPAC.

When you have finished this LIFEPAC, you should be able to:

1. Calculate gram-formula-weights.
2. Describe the three main characteristics of solutions.
3. Calculate molarity.
4. Define and identify ions.
5. Balance equations.
6. Apply the concepts of equilibrium to the dissolved-undissolved system.
7. Apply the *Law of Chemical Equilibrium* to the dissolved-undissolved system.
8. Predict if a precipitate will form given specific environments.
9. Describe the variables affecting the rate of dissolving.
10. Define and identify an acid.
11. Define and identify a base.
12. Describe neutralization.
13. Define and apply pH.
14. Apply equilibrium concepts to acid-base reactions.
15. Define and identify a salt.
16. Identify anions and cations.
17. Identify oxidizing and reducing agents.
18. Write half-reactions.
19. Balance redox reactions.

Survey the LIFEPAC. Ask yourself some questions about this study. Write your questions here.

_____

_____

_____

_____

_____

I. SOLUTIONS

Sodium chloride, sugar, glycerine, and water are four pure substances. Each is characterized by definite properties, such as vapor pressure, melting point, boiling point, density, crystalline shape, and so on. Suppose we mix some of these pure substances. Sodium chloride dissolves when placed in contact with water. The solid disappears and becomes part of the liquid. Likewise, sugar in contact with water dissolves. When glycerine is added to water, the two pure substances mix to give a liquid similar in appearance to the original liquids. The saltwater mixture, the sugar-water mixture, and the glycerine-water mixture are called solutions. They differ from pure substances in that their properties vary, depending upon the relative amounts of the constituents. The behavior of these solutions during phase changes is dramatically different from that just described for pure substances. These differences provide a basis for making a distinction between pure substances and solutions and a basis for deciding whether a given material is a pure substance or a solution. If you need more review of these ideas, restudy Science LIFEPAC 1102.

In this section you will review gram-formula-weights, moles, and equations; and you will learn about types and characteristics of solutions. Although many kinds of solutions exist, most of what you will study will involve water solutions. All of your study in this section will be a background for the next three sections of this LIFEPAC; therefore, study the first section carefully and thoroughly.

SECTION OBJECTIVES

Review these objectives. When you have completed this section, you should be able to:

1. Calculate gram-formula-weights.
2. Describe the three main characteristics of solutions.
3. Calculate molarity.
4. Define and identify ions.
5. Balance equations.

MOLES

You have learned that moles are units used to describe a certain fixed number of objects or items. Avogadro's Number, N, is used to define the number of objects in a mole. A mole is 6.02×10^{23} units, 22.4 liters of gas at STP, or one gram-formula-weight of any substance. The mass necessary to produce a mole is equal to the sum of atomic mass units (expressed in grams). The number of units in a mole is always the same, but the mass of a mole of one substance may vary from the mass of one mole of another substance.

This section of the LIFEPAC will review Science LIFEPAC 1103. If you are in doubt, review for added help.

Gram-formula-weight. Study the Periodic Table of Elements that came with Science LIFEPAC 1101. Also review pages 40 through 53 of Science LIFEPAC 1103. A mole of any substance is equal to the sum of the atomic masses of the elements in the substance expressed in grams.

Study the following examples.

The gram-formula-weight (g.f.w.) of NaOH is calculated:

1 – Na	=	23	grams/mole
1 – O	=	16	grams/mole
1 – H	=	1	gram/mole

NaOH	=	40	grams/mole = 1 g.f.w.

The gram-formula-weight of Na_2CO_3 is calculated:

2 – Na	=	46	grams/2 moles
1 – C	=	12	grams/mole
3 – O	=	48	grams/3 moles

Na_2CO_3	=	106	grams/mole = 1 g.f.w.

2

Complete these activities.

1.1   What is the atomic mass of one mole of Na?   _____

1.2   What is the atomic mass of one mole of H?   _____

1.3   What is the atomic mass of one mole of O?   _____

1.4   What is the g.f.w. of one mole of H_2O?   _____

1.5   What is the atomic mass of one mole of C?   _____

1.6   What is the g.f.w. of one mole of CO_2?   _____

1.7   What is the g.f.w. of one mole of $NaHCO_3$?   _____

1.8   What is the g.f.w. of one mole of H_2CO_3?   _____

1.9   What is the g.f.w. of one mole of CO?   _____

Balancing equations. A balanced equation is one that has the same number of atoms of each kind on both sides of the reaction. A balanced equation shows a Conservation of Mass. Review Science LIFEPAC 1103, pages 34 through 53, to refresh your memory on the techniques for balancing equations.

 Complete these activities.

1.10   Draw a circle around each coefficient (mole ratio number) and underline each subscript.

     a. $N_2 + 3\,H_2 \rightleftharpoons 2NH_3$

     b. $3\,Fe + 4\,H_2O \rightleftharpoons Fe_3O_4 + 4\,H_2$

1.11   Explain the meanings of each of the following equations.

     a. $Fe + S \rightleftharpoons FeS$ _____

     _____

     b. $2\,KClO_3 \rightleftharpoons 2\,KCl + 3\,O_2$ _____

     _____

     c. $CH_4 + 2\,O_2 \rightleftharpoons CO_2 + 2\,H_2O$ _____

     _____

1.12   In the following equations list the reactants and products.

     a. $2\,H_2 + O_2 \longrightarrow 2\,H_2O$ reactants: _____

                                       products: _____

     b. $2\,HgO \longrightarrow 2\,Hg + O_2$ reactants: _____

                                       products: _____

1.13   Balance the following equations.

     Reaction   **Balanced Equation**

     a. $H_2O \xrightarrow{\text{electric current}} H_2 + O_2$ a. _____

     b. $HCl + Zn \longrightarrow ZnCl_2 + H_2$ b. _____

     c. $H_2O_2 \longrightarrow H_2O + O_2$ c. _____

     d. $H_2 + CO \longrightarrow CH_3OH$ d. _____

     e. $Fe + O_2 \longrightarrow Fe_3O_4$ e. _____

     f. $Al + O_2 \longrightarrow Al_2O_3$ f. _____

     g. $NH_4OH + AlCl_3 \longrightarrow Al(OH)_3 + NH_4Cl$ g. _____

 Adult Check   _____

                     Initial   Date

Some parts of the earth are heterogeneous—they have many unlike parts. Some of the parts are uniform throughout—they are homogeneous. Familiar examples of heterogeneous materials are granite, which consists of various minerals suspended in another mineral; an oil and vinegar salad dressing, which consists of droplets of oil suspended in aqueous acetic acid; and black smoke, which consists of particles of soot suspended in air. Examples of homogeneous materials are diamond, water, saltwater, and clear air. Heterogeneous materials are hard to describe and classify but we can describe homogeneous materials rather precisely.

Pure substances and solutions are both homogeneous. A homogeneous material that contains only one substance is called a pure substance. A solution is a homogeneous material that contains more than one substance.

We have used the terms gas phase, liquid phase, and solid phase. A phase is a homogeneous part of a system—a part that is uniform and alike throughout. A system is any region, and the material in that region is that which we wish to consider. A system may include only one phase or more than one phase. For a further review of solutions, reread Science LIFEPAC 1102.

Gaseous solutions. All gas mixtures are homogeneous, hence all gas mixtures are solutions. Air is an example. Air is only one phase—the gas phase—and all the molecules, whatever the source, behave as gas molecules. The molecules themselves may have come from gaseous substances, liquid substances, or solid substances. Whatever the source of the constituents, this gaseous solution, air, is a single, homogeneous phase. As with other solutions the constituents of air are separated by phase changes.

Solid solutions. Solid solutions are more rare. Crystals are stable because of the regularity of the positioning of the atoms. A foreign atom interferes with this regularity and decreases the stability of the crystal. Therefore, as a crystal forms, it tends to exclude foreign atoms. Crystallization, as a result, provides a good method for purification of substances from a mixture.

Only in metals are solid solutions relatively common. The atoms of one element may enter the crystal of another element if their atoms have similar size. Gold and copper form such solid solutions. The gold atoms can replace copper atoms in the copper crystal, and in the same way copper atoms can replace gold atoms in the gold crystal. Such solid solutions are called *alloys*. Some solid metals dissolve hydrogen or carbon atoms. For example, steel is iron containing a small amount of dissolved carbon.

Liquid solutions. In your laboratory work you will deal mostly with liquid solutions. Liquid solutions can be made by mixing two liquids (for example, water and glycerine), by dissolving a gas in a liquid (for example, carbon dioxide and water), or by dissolving a solid in a liquid (for example, sugar and water). The result is a homogeneous system containing more than one substance: a solution. In such a liquid each component is diluted by the other component. In saltwater the salt dilutes the water and the water dilutes the salt. The solution is only partly made up of water molecules and the vapor pressure of the solution is correspondingly lower than the vapor pressure of pure water. Whereas water must be heated to 100°C to raise the vapor pressure to 760 mm, a salt solution must be heated above 100°C to reach this vapor pressure. Therefore, the boiling point of saltwater is above the boiling point of pure water. The amount the boiling point is raised depends upon the relative amounts of water and salt. As more salt is added, the boiling point increases.

In a similar way, a lower temperature is required to crystallize ice from saltwater or from a glycerine/water solution than from pure water. "Antifreeze" substances added to automobile radiators act on this principle—they dilute the water in the radiator and lower the temperature at which ice can crystallize from the solution. Putting salt on ice around the container of an ice cream freezer lowers the freezing point of the ice-water bath so that the ice cream freezes. Again the amount that the freezing temperature is lowered depends upon the relative amounts of water and the "antifreeze" compound.

In general, the properties of a solution depend upon the relative amounts of the components. We should be able to specify quantitatively what is present in a solution, that is, to specify its composition. The composition of a solution can be specified in many ways, but one method will suffice for our purposes.

Answer *true* or *false*.

1.14 _____ All gaseous mixtures are solutions.

1.15 _____ Solid solutions are common.

1.16 _____ Vapor pressure of water is not affected by the amount of salt added.

1.17 _____ Alloys are examples of solid solutions.

1.18 _____ Crystallization is a good way to purify solids.

1.19 _____ Salt acts as an antifreeze.

CHARACTERISTICS

The components of a solution are the pure substances that are mixed to form the solution. If the solution contains two components, one is sometimes called the *solvent* and the other the *solute*. These terms are used merely for convenience. Since both must intermingle to form the final solution, we cannot make any important distinction between them. When chemists make a liquid solution from a pure liquid and a solid, they usually call the liquid component the solvent.

Concentrations. To indicate the composition of a particular solution, we must show the relative amounts as well as the kind of components. These relative amounts chemists call *concentrations*. Chemists use different ways of expressing concentration for various purposes. You will study two different ways to calculate concentrations in this LIFEPAC, one in this section and one in the third section.

Chemists often indicate the concentration of a substance in water solution by the number of moles dissolved per liter of solution. This concentration is called the molar concentration. A one-molar (1 M) solution contains one mole of the solute per liter of total solution, a 2-molar solution (2 M) contains two moles of solute per liter, and a 0.1-molar solution (0.1 M) contains one-tenth mole of solute per liter.

Notice that the concentration of water is not specified though we must add definite amounts of water to make the definite amounts of solutions.

If you add two lumps of sugar to a cup of coffee, it is twice as sweet as with one lump; but just how concentrated is this sugar solution? The simplest way to express concentration is to use the moles of substance dissolved in one liter of solution. This measure is defined as *molarity*, or moles per liter of solution. You will note that *molarity* and *molar concentration* both refer to the same thing. Let's investigate this idea of molarity (M) using a salt (NaCl) solution.

We can make a 1 M solution of sodium chloride by weighing out one mole of the salt. From the formula, NaCl, we know that one mole weighs 58.5 g (23.0 g + 35.5 g). We dissolve this salt in some water in a flask holding just one liter when filled exactly to an etched mark. After the salt dissolves, more water is added until the water level reaches the etched mark to make the volume exactly one liter. We could prepare a 1 M sodium chloride solution by using a 100 ml volumetric flask. Then the final volume of the solution would be 0.100 liter, and the amount of salt needed would be only one-tenth of a mole. In this last case, we would weigh out 5.85 g of salt, place it in the flask, dissolve it, and add water to the 100 ml mark.

Do these activities.

1.20 The g.f.w. of NaCl is 58.5 grams/mole. If you had a 1-molar solution (1 M) you would have to put 58.5 g of salt in 1 liter of solution.

$$1 \text{ M NaCl} = \frac{1 \text{ mole}}{\text{liter}} = \frac{1 \text{ g.f.w.}}{1 \text{ liter}} = \frac{1 \text{ g.f.w.}}{1{,}000 \text{ ml}} = \frac{58.5 \text{ g NaCl}}{1 \text{ liter}} = \frac{58.5 \text{ g NaCl}}{1{,}000 \text{ ml}}$$

a. How many moles of NaCl would you have in 100 ml? _____

b. This would equal _____ grams.

5

1.21   Suppose that instead of a 1 M solution you decided to make up a 0.5 M solution.

a. How many moles of NaCl would there be in one liter? _____

b. In 1,000 ml? _____

c. You would need to have _____ grams of NaCl in 1,000 ml.

d. How many grams would there be in 10 ml? _____

1.22   Now dilute 10 ml of the 0.5 M NaCl by adding distilled water until 100 ml of solution are produced.

a. Does the diluted NaCl have more, less, or the same "saltiness" as the original 10 ml of 0.5 M NaCl? _____

b. Has the concentration of the diluted salt solution increased, decreased, or remained constant? _____

c. Has the actual amount of dissolved salt increased, decreased, or remained the same? _____

d. When a solution is diluted, does the dilution change the number of grams dissolved? _____

e. When a solution is diluted, does it change the number of moles dissolved? _____

f. Does dilution change the concentration? _____

Adult Check   _____
                Initial   Date

Do these activities.

1.23   From the calculations in 1.22, complete this activity.

+90 ml
H₂O

10 ml diluted to 100 ml

a. _____   0.5 M NaCl ⟶ _____   M NaCl
b. _____   moles NaCl ⟶ _____   moles NaCl
c. _____   grams NaCl ⟶ _____   grams NaCl

1.24   Recheck your ideas about concentrations of solutions by doing the following exercise. Use a 0.2 M NaCl as the solution this time.

?

$$0.2 \text{ M} \longrightarrow 0.04 \text{ M}$$

a. _____   10 ml ml $\longrightarrow$ _____ ml

b. _____   moles $\longrightarrow$ _____ moles

c. _____   grams NaCl $\longrightarrow$ _____ grams NaCl

☑ **Adult Check**   _____

                       Initial   Date

1.25   Look again at 1.22. The initial amount of salt solution (10 ml) and concentration (0.5 M) were given.

      a. If you multiply these two values, (10 ml) (0.5 M), their product is _____ .

      b. Do the same thing for the diluted solution.

         _____ ml x _____ M = _____

      c. What do you discover about the two numbers you have just calculated?

         _____

      d. Determine whether this concept is true for 1.24 also. Proof:

         _____ x _____ = _____ x _____

> A general formula for this relationship can be written:
>
> (initial concentration) (initial volume) = (final concentration) (final volume)

1.26   Calculate the molarity of the following solutions:

      a. 4.32×10^2 moles of CH_3COOH in 20.0 liters.   _____

      b. 29 g of NaCl (g.f.w. = 58) in 0.25 liters.   _____

      c. 100 g of $C_{12}H_{22}O_{11}$ (g.f.w. = 342) in 1.15 liters.   _____

      d. 6.02×10^{22} molecules of HCl (g.f.w. = 36.5) in 2 liters. _____

Choose the correct answer.

1.27   To make a salt solution twice as concentrated you could _____ .

      a. add twice as much salt   d. a, b, and c

      b. add twice as much water   e. a and c

      c. evaporate off half the water   f. a and b

☑ **Adult Check**   _____

                       Initial   Date

Electrical nature. Concentration is one factor that affects the characteristics of a solution. The second factor is the electrical nature of solvent and solute. You have learned that all matter is made up of electrons, protons, and neutrons. When the number of electrons is unequal to the number of protons, the particle is called an *ion*. (Review Science LIFEPAC 1104.)

In a solution, ions act as "carriers" of electrical charge. When an electrical current is passed through a solution, a greater number of ions provides greater conductivity of the solution. In other words, a greater number of "carriers" (ions), permits more electricity to go through a solution. Now you will study a second factor determining the number of ions in solution: electrical nature. Study the apparatus as pictured in Figure 1. Results for

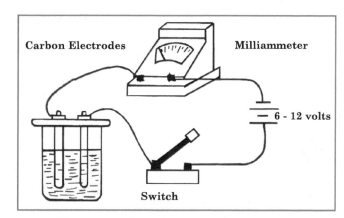

FIGURE 1: CONDUCTIVITY APPARATUS

the test solutions are recorded in Data Table 1. Study the results carefully. Look for a pattern in the data.

DATA TABLE 1

Solution	Meter Reading	1.30 Bond Type (ionic or covalent)
0.01 M NaCl	100. ma.	a.
CCl₄	0. ma.	b.
Distilled H₂O	0. ma.	c.
Tap H₂O	2. ma.	d.
0.01 M Sucrose (C₁₂H₂₂O₁₁)	0. ma.	e.
0.01 M KCl	110. ma.	f.
0.01 M HCl	110. ma.	g.

Ionic compounds are those that are composed of ions. Covalent compounds are composed of atoms that are held together by the mutual attraction to each other's single unshared valence electrons. (Review Science LIFEPAC 1105). Ionic compounds only have to dissociate or break apart from the already formed ionic crystals. An example is

$$\text{Na}^+ \text{Cl}^-_{(s)} \xrightarrow{\text{H}_2\text{O}} \text{Na}^+_{(aq)} + \text{Cl}^-_{(aq)}$$

However, covalent molecules generally dissolve as molecules rather than ions. Sucrose is an example. If covalent molecules do dissolve to form conducting solutions, they must first ionize. Ionization is the process of a molecule forming ions. Hydrochloric acid, HCl, is an example of a covalent molecule ionizing in water to form ions.

$$\text{HCl}_{(g)} \xrightarrow{\text{H}_2\text{O}} \text{H}^+_{(aq)} + \text{Cl}^-_{(aq)}$$

Covalent molecules take more energy to dissolve because they must both ionize and dissociate, both steps consuming energy.

What is different about the electrical nature of matter, especially covalent compounds, to cause the difference in conductivity? The next activities will help you answer that question.

8

Complete these activities.

1.28 Which of these solutions will be the best conductor of electricity? _____

(Any water solution that conducts electricity is called an electrolyte.)

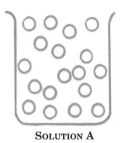

O = Neutral particles

+ = Positive ions

- = Negative ions

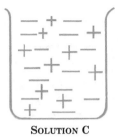

SOLUTION A   SOLUTION B   SOLUTION C

1.29 Circle the letters for all the ions in the following list.

a. NO_2 d. Cu   g. Mg   j. HSO_4^{-1}

b. SO_4 e. PO_4^{-3} h. H^+ k. H_2O

c. Al^{+3} f. SO_2 i. $HC_2H_3O_2$ l. H_3O^{+1}

1.30 Determine the ionic-covalent nature of the compounds listed in Data Table 1. Use Science LIFEPAC 1105 and the Periodic Table as references and record the percent ionic character of compounds in the list. (See Data Table 1.)

1.31 Look carefully at Data Table 1.

a. Do solutions and liquids of ionic or covalent character tend to conduct electricity best?

_____

b. Therefore, do ionic or covalent substances tend to produce more ions in solution?

_____

c. Do ionic substances dissociate or ionize while dissolving? _____

d. Do covalent substances dissociate or ionize while dissolving? _____

e. Which requires more energy to dissolve, ionic or covalent compounds? _____

f. When the percent ionic character increases, the conductivity _____ .

HCl dissolves in water to form an ionic solution. What about other covalent molecules? Why do some ionize while others do not? Seven clean test tubes with seven stoppers to fit were set up. The following procedure was used with each solution. A record of the observations is given in Data Table 2.

The student:

1. Used 2 ml H_2O and 5 drops of CCl_4 and shook the test tube.
2. Used 2 ml H_2O and 5 drops of C_6H_6 and shook the test tube.
3. Used 2 ml CCl_4 and 5 drops of C_6H_6 and shook the test tube.
4. Used 2 ml H_2O and 1 crystal of I_2 and shook the test tube.
5. Used 2 ml CCl_4 and 1 crystal of I_2 and shook the test tube.
6. Used 2 ml CCl_4 and 5 drops of C_2H_5OH and shook the test tube.
7. Used 2 ml H_2O and 5 drops of C_2H_5OH and shook the test tube.

Test Tube	Observations	1.32 Complete for Each Test		
1	Did CCl_4 dissolve? **No**	a. Is CCl_4 covalent? _____ Polar? _____ b. Is H_2O covalent? _____ Polar? _____		
2	Did C_6H_6 dissolve? **No**	c. Is H_2O covalent? _____ Polar? _____ d. Is C_6H_6 covalent? _____ Polar? _____		
3	Did C_6H_6 dissolve? **Yes**	e. Is CCl_4 covalent? _____ Polar? _____ f. Is C_6H_6 covalent? _____ Polar? _____		
4	Did I_2 dissolve? **No**	g. Is I_2 covalent? _____ Polar? _____ h. Is H_2O covalent? _____ Polar? _____		
5	Did I_2 dissolve? **Yes**	i. Is I_2 covalent? _____ Polar? _____ j. Is CCl_4 covalent? _____ Polar? _____		
6	Did C_2H_5OH dissolve? **No**	k. Is C_2H_5OH covalent? _____ Polar? _____ l. Is CCl_4 covalent? _____ Polar? _____		
7	Did C_2H_5OH dissolve? **Yes**	m. Is C_2H_5OH covalent? _____ Polar? _____ n. Is H_2O covalent? _____ Polar? _____		

Complete these activities.

1.32   Using Science LIFEPAC 1105 and the Periodic Table, complete Data Table 2.

1.33   Study from Data Table 2.

a. Do polar molecules dissolve in polar liquids? _____

b. Do nonpolar molecules dissolve in nonpolar liquids?_____

c. Do polar molecules dissolve in nonpolar liquids? _____

d. How do you explain the phrase "Like dissolves like"? _____

_____

_____

e. Why is grease removed better with CCl_4 than with H_2O? _____

_____

_____

f. Why does HCl ionize better in H_2O than in C_6H_6? _____

_____

_____

1.34   A chemistry student carried out an experiment with a conducting apparatus similar to the one in Figure 1. The following data was taken.

Solution	Reading
0.1 M H_2SO_4	150 ma.
0.1 M $Ba(OH)_2$	150 ma.

a. Does the $Ba(OH)_2$ solution contain ions? _____

b. Does the H_2SO_4 solution contain ions? _____

1.35   To 30 ml of the $Ba(OH)_2$ solution, 10 ml portions of H_2SO_4 were added until a total of 50 ml of H_2SO_4 were used. The following results were recorded.

DATA TABLE 3

Total H_2SO_4 Added	Meter Reading	Observations
0 ml	150 ma.	Ba $(OH)_2$ and H_2SO_4 clear, colorless
10 ml	65 ma.	milky white precipitate forms
20 ml	31 ma.	more precipitate forms
30 ml	0 ma.	precipitate heavy and settles
40 ml	29 ma.	no added precipitate seen to form
50 ml	62 ma.	no change seen

Plot the meter reading on the graph provided. Be sure to properly label the axes.

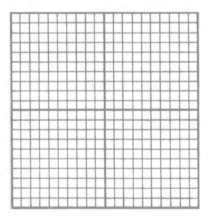

1.36   Explain the data.

a. Is any evidence shown that a reaction has occurred? _____

b. Does the conductivity increase or decrease? _____

_____

c. Does the number of ions in solution increase, decrease, or remain constant?

_____

d. How can you tell? _____

_____

11

e. How does this evidence indicate that the reaction has occurred between ions?

_____

_____

_____

f. The $Ba(OH)_2$ dissociates as $Ba^{+2} + 2 OH^-$. H_2SO_4 dissociates as $2 H^+ + SO_4^{-2}$. Write a balanced equation for this reaction. _____

_____

g. When the conductivity is at a minimum, what must be true about the amount of $Ba(OH)_2$ compared to H_2SO_4? _____

h. Why does it not conduct at this low point? _____

_____

_____

i. Why does it conduct more before and after this minimum point? _____

_____

_____

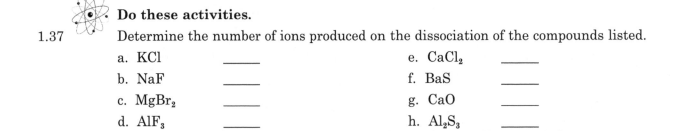

Adult Check   _____
                        Initial   Date

Potential number of ions. We now have studied two characteristics of solutions, molarity and electrical nature of the solute and solvent. The third factor is the potential number of ions available in the solute to dissociate, or to ionize, to carry the current. For example, when NaCl dissociates to form separate Na^+ and Cl^- ions in solution, the total number of potential ions is two. When $MgCl_2$ dissociates, the potential number of ions is three ($MgCl_2 \longrightarrow Mg^{+2} + Cl^- + Cl^-$). The dissociation of $AlCl_3$ produces four ions ($AlCl_3 \longrightarrow Al^{+3} + Cl^- + Cl^- + Cl^-$). Therefore, one mole of NaCl produces two moles of ions; one mole of $MgCl_2$ produces three moles of ions; and one mole of $AlCl_3$ produces four moles of ions.

Study Data Table 4. You should become very familiar with these common ions before you finish this section. Memorizing the list for future reference would be to your advantage.(Review Science LIFEPAC 1105, Section I, before you go on.) This review section states that when ions combine, the product is electrically neutral. For example, when NH_4^+ reacts with OH^- the product is NH_4OH. When NH_4^+ reacts with PO_4^{-3} the product is $(NH_4)_3PO_4$. The dissociation, or ionization, process is the reverse of the formation process. For example, $(NH_4)_3PO_4 \rightleftharpoons 3 NH_4^+ + PO_4^{-3}$. The number of potential ions in a complex compound can be determined from the formation process. Multi-atom ions tend to remain together and act as single ions in the dissociation or ionization process.

Do these activities.

1.37   Determine the number of ions produced on the dissociation of the compounds listed.

a. KCl   _____   e. $CaCl_2$ _____

b. NaF   _____   f. BaS   _____

c. $MgBr_2$ _____   g. CaO   _____

d. AlF_3 _____   h. Al_2S_3 _____

DATA TABLE 4

NAMES, FORMULAS, AND CHANGES OF SOME COMMON IONS

Positive Ions (Cations)

Name	Formula	Name	Formula
Aluminum	Al^{+3}	Lithium	Li^+
Ammonium	NH_4^+	Magnesium	Mg^{+2}
Barium	Ba^{+2}	Manganese (II) Manganous	Mn^{+2}
Calcium	Ca^{+2}	Mercury (I) Mercurous	Hg_2^{+2}
Chromium (III) Chromic	Cr^{+3}	Mercury (II) Mercuric	Hg^{+2}
Copper (I) Cuprous	Cu^+	Potassium	K^+
Copper (II) Cupric	Cu^{+2}	Silver	Ag^+
Hydrogen	H^+	Sodium	Na^+
Iron (II) Ferrous	Fe^{+2}	Tin (II) Stannous	Sn^{+2}
Iron (III) Ferric	Fe^{+3}	Tin (IV) Stannic	Sn^{+4}
Lead	Pb^{+2}	Zinc	Zn^{+2}

Negative Ions (Anions)

Name	Formula	Name	Formula
Acetate	CH_3COO^-	Nitrite	NO_2^-
Bromide	Br^-	Oxalate	$C_2O_4^{-2}$
Carbonate	CO_3^{-2}	Hydrogen Oxalate ion (Binoxalate)	$HC_2O_4^-$
Hydrogen Carbonate ion (Bicarbonate)	HCO_3^-	Perchlorate	ClO_4^-
Chlorate	ClO_3^-	Permanganate	MnO_4^-
Chloride	Cl^-	Phosphate	PO_4^{-3}
Chlorite	ClO_2^-	Monohydrogen Phosphate	HPO_4^{-2}
Chromate	CrO_4^{-2}	Dihydrogen Phosphate	$H_2PO_4^-$
Dichromate	$Cr_2O_7^{-2}$	Sulfate	SO_4^{-2}
Fluoride	F^-	Hydrogen Sulfate ion (Bisulfate)	HSO_4^-
Hydroxide	OH^-	Sulfide	S^{-2}
Hypochlorite	ClO^-	Hydrogen Sulfide ion (Bisulfide)	HS^-
Iodide	I^-	Sulfite	SO_3^{-2}
Nitrate	NO_3^-	Hydrogen Sulfite ion (Bisulfite)	HSO_3^-

1.38   Predict the formulas of the ion pairs listed.

      a. NH_4^+, CO_3^{-2} _____

      b. lead, iodide   _____

      c. H^+, SO_4^{-2} _____

      d. calcium, hydroxide   _____

      e. Na^+, OH^- _____

      f. zinc, oxalate   _____

      g. tin (IV), sulfate   _____

      h. silver, nitrate   _____

1.39   Predict the potential number of ions for each compound listed in 1.38.

      a. _____   e. _____

      b. _____   f. _____

      c. _____   g. _____

      d. _____   h. _____

Adult Check   _____

                  Initial   Date

Review the material in this section in preparation for the Self Test. The Self Test will check your mastery of this particular section. The items missed on this Self Test will indicate specific areas where restudy is needed for mastery.

Use the Periodic Table of Elements that came with Science LIFEPAC 1101 as necessary.

Choose the correct answer (each answer, 3 points).

1.01   Circle all the species that are ions.

      a. HCl
                    d. NaCl

      b. NH_4^+
                 e. $H_2PO_4^-$

      c. CCl_4
                  f. H_3O^+

1.02   Both members of each pair are very soluble in water. If you had equal molar concentrations of each solution, which member of each pair would theoretically be the better conductor of electricity? (Circle one member of each pair.)

      a. $CsCl$, $CaCl_2$
               d. CaS, Li_2S

      b. KBr, $AlCl_3$
             e. $AlCl_3$, $MgCl_2$

      c. KI, K_2S

1.03   Which 0.1 M solution out of each group would conduct the most electricity?

      a. CsF, NaCl, KBr
              c. sucrose, glycerine, KI

      b. $NaBr$, KCl, $AlCl_3$, $MgCl_2$

1.04   Which of the following choices would be a nonconducting substance or solution (more than one may be correct).

      a. carbon tetrachloride
         d. $CaCl_2$ (dissolved in water)

      b. BeF_2 (dissolved in water)
      e. BaF_2 (dissolved in water)

      c. distilled water

1.05   Which solution of NaI would conduct the most current?

      a. 0.1 M
          b. 0.8 M
          c. 0.3 M
          d. 0.6 M

1.06   What relationship seems to be true concerning electronegativity of different species?

      a. When ionic character increases electrical conductivity decreases.

      b. When ionic character decreases electrical conductivity decreases.

      c. When ionic character decreases electrical conductivity increases.

      d. When ionic character increases electrical conductivity stays the same.

1.07   Which of the following ionic compounds when prepared as equal molar solutions would be the best conductor of electricity?

      a. BeF_2
          c. $CaBr_2$
          e. $CaCl_2$

      b. SrF_2
          d. $BaBr_2$

1.08   From the following pairs of substances, select which of the substances is more likely to be soluble in water. (Circle one in each pair.)

      a. O_2 or NH_3
         d. I_2 or NaI
         g. CCl_4 or NH_3

      b. CF_4 or CH_2F_2
      e. $NaCl$ or CCl_4
      h. NaF or $AlCl_3$

      c. H_2S or CH_4
      f. NH_3 or PH_3
      i. $BrCl$ or CCl_4

Make these calculations (each answer, 5 points).

1.09   Determine the g.f.w. of H_2O.

1.010   Determine the g.f.w. of $Ca_3(PO_4)_2$.

Potassium fluoride (KF), a salt, has a gram-formula-weight of 58 grams. Answer the following questions based on this data. Show your work in the space provided and place your answers on the lines at the left.

1.011   How many grams would be needed to mix 1 liter of 5.0 molar salt solution?

            _____

1.012   How many grams would be needed to mix 1 liter of 0.1 M salt solution?

            _____

Answer *true* **or** *false* (each answer, 1 point).

1.013   _____   Like dissolves like.
1.014   _____   Ions can be made of more than one atom.
1.015   _____   Molecules are charged.
1.016   _____   Liquid solutions are rare to find.
1.017   _____   Ions are electrically neutral.
1.018   _____   Salt acts as an antifreeze.

Complete these statements (each answer, 3 points).

1.019   The three factors that determine the characteristics of a solution are:

            a. _____ ,
            b. _____ , and
            c. _____ .

1.020   The liquid component that makes up the largest part of a solution is called the

            a. _____ , and the substance that is dissolved is called the
            b. _____ .

Balance these equations (each answer, 3 points).

1.021   _____ H_2 + _____ O_2 ⟶ _____ H_2O
1.022   _____ $Pb(NO_3)_2$ + _____ NaI ⟶ _____ PbI_2 + _____ $NaNO_3$

Score   _____
Adult check   _____
                     Initial   Date

16

II. SOLUBILITY EQUILIBRIUMS

In Science LIFEPAC 1106 you studied the concept of equilibrium. You learned that an equilibrium condition was a dynamic system in which the rate of reaction in one direction was equal to the rate of reaction in the opposite direction (reactants $\rightleftharpoons$ products). The building process was equal to the decaying process.

You also found that the mathematical expression for a chemical equilibrium was given by the following expression:

$$aA + bB \rightleftharpoons cC + dD \qquad K_{eq} = \frac{[C]^c[D]^d}{[A]^a[B]^b}$$

In the next three sections of this LIFEPAC, you will study specific types of equilibrium systems. In this section you will study systems in which a solid is in equilibrium with its dissolved form. Some practical applications of the concepts of this section will be used to show you the importance of this study. Review Section III of Science LIFEPAC 1106 for further reference.

SECTION OBJECTIVES

Review these objectives. When you have completed this section, you should be able to:

6. Apply the concepts of equilibrium to the dissolved-undissolved system.

7. Apply the *Law of Chemical Equilibrium* to the dissolved-undissolved system.

8. Predict if a precipitate will form given specific environments.

9. Describe the variables affecting the rate of dissolving.

DISSOLVING AND DISSOCIATING

The formation of a solution occurs in two steps. The first is the separation of the solute into ions or molecules and the second is the diffusion of the solute throughout the solvent. The second step was discussed in depth in a previous LIFEPAC. If you need to refresh your memory on the kinetics of diffusion, review pages 2 and 3 of Science LIFEPAC 1103.

Definition. Dissolving and dissociating is the mechanical separation of the ions or molecules that make up the solute. Study Figure 2. Notice that when dissolving starts, all of the solute particles move away from the solute source. After a little time, the concentration of the solute particles around the source has increased to a level where some of the solute particles randomly hit the source and reattach themselves to the source. The net result is still more movement away from the solute source than back to the source. The attraction of the solvent for solute particles and the diffusion-dilution process cause the dissolving to proceed away from the solute source until an equilibrium is established.

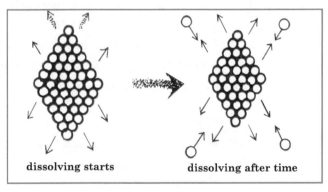

dissolving starts   dissolving after time

FIGURE 2

 Complete these statements.

2.1   A solution is formed by the processes of a. _____ and b. _____ .

2.2   The substance that is dissolving is called the _____ .

2.3   The process of intermingling of the ions (molecules) of one substance into another is called
_____

2.4   Dissolving continues until an _____ is reached.

2.5   The dissolving process is primarily _____ the solute when the dissolving begins.

Factors affecting rate. A solution is a homogeneous mixture of two or more substances. The composition of a solution may vary within certain limits. Varying amounts of solute may be dissolved and varying amounts of solvent may be used. The solution process and those physical factors that affect it will be studied in the next investigations.

The factors affecting the rate of dissolving/dissociation will be investigated by the inductive approach. You will explore the factors and from your results develop your ideas and generalizations. The following materials will be used to investigate all four factors.

Do these investigations.

> **These supplies are needed:**
>
>   rock salt (water softener crystals)   glycerine
>   water   2 baby-food jars with lids
>   rubbing alcohol (isopropyl alcohol)   stirring rod
>   test tubes

Follow these directions and complete these activities. Put a check in the box when each step is completed.

Effect of solvent

❏ 1. Place 2 ml of water in a test tube, 2 ml of alcohol in a second test tube, and 2 ml of glycerine in a third test tube.

❏ 2. Label each to avoid confusion.

❏ 3. Drop a crystal of NaCl into each test tube.

❏ 4. Shake each test tube gently for about one minute.

2.6   What results?

     a. H_2O = _____

     b. alcohol = _____

     c. glycerine = _____

2.7   In which liquid is the salt most soluble? _____

2.8   Using the concept of "Like dissolves like," explain why you got the results you did in 2.6.

_____

_____

2.9   Explain how the choice of solvent affects the dissolving process.

_____

_____

_____

18

Effect of pulverizing

- ❏ 5. Weigh out two 2 g portions of coarse crystals.
- ❏ 6. Grind one portion to a fine powder, but do not pound the crystals.
- ❏ 7. Place the finely ground crystals into one baby-food jar and the coarse crystals into a second baby-food jar.
- ❏ 8. Now add 25 ml of water to each baby food jar. Put lids on both jars.
- ❏ 9. Simultaneously agitate the two jars with a swirling motion.
- ❏ 10. Observe the time required for complete solution in each jar.

2.10   Record of dissolving times.

a. crystal = _____

b. pulverized = _____

2.11   Why are the dissolving rates different? _____

_____

_____

_____

_____

Effect of temperature

- ❏ 11. Weigh out two 2 g portions of coarse salt crystals.
- ❏ 12. Place one 2 g sample in each of two baby food jars.
- ❏ 13. Measure out 25 ml of ice water and 25 ml of hot water.
- ❏ 14. Pour the cold water in one jar and the hot water in the second jar.
- ❏ 15. Put lids on both jars.
- ❏ 16. Wrap the hot jar in paper or cloth to keep it hot and to avoid a burn to your hand.
- ❏ 17. Simultaneously agitate the jars, recording the time required to dissolve each 2 g sample.

2.12   Record of dissolving times.

a. cold = _____

b. hot = _____

2.13   Using the concepts of kinetic energy, describe why you found the results you did in 2.12.

_____

_____

_____

_____

_____

Effect of stirring.

- ❏ 18. Weigh out two 2 g portions of coarse salt crystals.
- ❏ 19. Put each salt sample in a separate baby food jar.
- ❏ 20. Add 25 ml of tap water to each sample.
- ❏ 21. Stir one sample and leave the second sample unstirred. Record the times necessary to dissolve each sample.

2.14   Record of dissolving time.

        a. stirred = _____

        b. unstirred = _____

2.15   Explain the results recorded in 2.14. _____

        _____

        _____

2.16   Review the four factors of dissolving you have just investigated. Given the correct solvent for a solute, what could you do to hasten the solution process?

        1. _____

        2. _____

        3. _____

 Adult Check   _____

                      Initial   Date

SOLUBILITY CONSTANTS

When a solution reaches a point where the rate of dissolving equals the rate of reforming (solidification), the system is in equilibrium (dissolved $\rightleftharpoons$ undissolved). This equilibrium system is the one you will study in this section of your LlFEPAC.

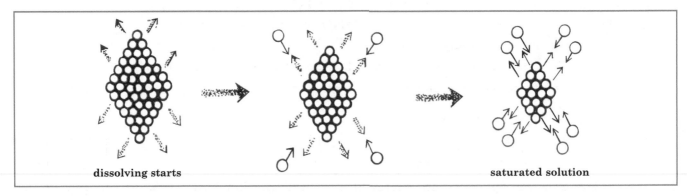

dissolving starts   saturated solution

Ksp. In your study of Science LIFEPAC 1106, you were introduced to the general concepts involved in equilibrium. The Law of Chemical Equilibrium was described as

$$aA + bB \rightleftharpoons cC + dD \qquad K_{eq} = \frac{[C]^c[D]^d}{[A]^a[B]^b}.$$

You will now learn to apply the equilibrium law to the equilibrium system of a saturated solution in which a solid is in equilibrium with its dissolved form.

 Do these activities.

2.17   Our laboratory studies will be based upon the system of $PbCl_{2(s)} \rightleftharpoons Pb^{+2}_{(aq)} + 2Cl^-_{(aq)}$.

        a. For every Pb^{+2} ion that is formed, how many Cl^- ions are formed? _____

        b. For every mole of Pb^{+2} ions that are formed, how many moles of Cl^- ions are formed? _____

The following experiment was carried out by a chemistry student. The directions and data are given for your reference.

Directions:

Place 100 ml of filtered PbCl₂ (saturated solution) in a 150 ml beaker. Wash a spiral Al wire in acetone to remove the dirt and grease. Weigh the Al wire and place it in the PbCl₂ solution so that one end is hooked over the rim of the beaker. As the lead begins to form on the wire, shake it off. Allow the system to stand overnight. Rinse off all of the lead from the wire. Filter, wash, dry, and weigh the lead formed and Al wire left. Record the data in Data Table 5.

DATA TABLE 5

Weight of Al wire before =		3.96 g
Weight of Al wire after =		3.65 g
a.	Weight of Al lost =	
b.	Moles of Al lost =	
	Weight of Pb + filter paper =	4.26 g
	Weight of filter paper =	0.92 g
c.	Weight of Pb =	
d.	Moles of Pb formed =	

2.18   Complete Data Table 5.

2.19   Analyze Data Table 5.

    a. What are the units used to express concentration? _____

    b. When [ ] are around an ion, what does it represent? _____

2.20   What is the [Pb⁺²] for the saturated solution of PbCl₂? _____

2.21   What is the [Cl⁻] for the saturated solution of PbCl₂? _____

2.22   The symbol model for the reaction between Al and Pb^{+2} is $2\ Al° + 3\ Pb^{+2} \rightleftharpoons 2\ Al^{+3} + 3\ Pb°$

    a. Therefore, for each two moles of Al that are used, how many moles of Pb° are formed?

    _____

    b. From the moles of Al lost, calculate the number of moles of Pb° that should have been formed.

2.23   Calculate [Pb⁺²] based upon the amount of Al lost. _____

2.24   Calculate the [Cl⁻] based upon the amount Al lost. _____

To verify the previous experiment the chemistry student carried out the next experiment and recorded the data for you in Data Table 6.

Directions:

Place 100 ml of filtered PbCl₂ in a 150 ml beaker and put it under the dryer to evaporate the water. Record the necessary data in Data Table 6.

DATA TABLE 6

Weight of beaker + PbCl₂ =	62.19 g
Weight of beaker =	57.77 g
a. Weight of $PbCl_2$ per 100 ml =	
b. Moles $PbCl_2$ per 100 ml =	
c. $[Pb^{+2}]$ based upon this investigation =	
d. $[Cl^-]$ based upon this investigation =	

2.25   Complete Data Table 6.

 Adult Check _____

                    Initial   Date

The equilibrium expression K_{eq} for this system is written:

$$K_{eq} = \frac{[Pb^{+2}][Cl^-]^2}{[PbCl_{2(s)}]}$$

The crystalline concentration of the $PbCl_{2(s)}$ is found to be always a constant and can be represented by k_1.

The K_{eq} expression can be written:

$$K_{eq} = \frac{[Pb^{+2}][Cl^-]^2}{k_1}$$

$$K_{eq} \times k_1 = [Pb^{+2}][Cl^-]^2 = K_{sp}$$

$$K_{sp} = [Pb^{+2}][Cl^-]^2$$

The constant K_{sp} is called the *solubility product* constant. In any saturated solution the K_{sp} is used to represent the numerical value of the equilibrium expression.

 Do these activities.

2.26   Determine the K_{sp} values of $PbCl_2$ for the three methods used in the previous investigation.

    a. Based upon lead formed data (2.20 and 2.21):

       K_{sp} = _____

    b. Based upon Al lost data (2.23 and 2.24):

       K_{sp} = _____

    c. Based upon dried $PbCl_2$ data (2.25):

       K_{sp} = _____

2.27   From a handbook of chemical data the student found the K_{sp} value for $PbCl_2$ to be 1.8×10^{-2}. Discuss why the accepted value may be different from the experimental values determined in 2.26.

    a. _____

    b. _____

    c. _____

2.28   A K_{sp} of 1 x 10^{-2} might be considered to mean a small degree of solubility.

   a. From the size of the $PbCl_2$ K_{sp} value, do you think that the reactant or the products are favored in this system? _____

   b. Explain. _____
   _____
   _____
   _____
   _____

2.29   Draw an enthalpy diagram which you think represents this equilibrium system.

2.30   What is a saturated solution of $PbCl_2$? ($PbCl_{2(s)} \rightleftharpoons Pb^{+2} + 2 Cl^-$)

   _____
   _____
   _____
   _____

2.31   The student placed 10 ml of $PbCl_2$ (saturated solution) in the test tube and added a pinch of NaCl. A white precipitate of $PbCl_2$ formed.

   a. Have you increased or decreased the Cl^- concentration by adding NaCl? _____

   b. According to Le Chatelier's Principle, why did the added Cl^- cause the precipitate of $PbCl_2$ to form? _____
   _____
   _____

2.32   The student placed 10 ml of $PbCl_2$ (saturated solution) in a test tube and added a pinch of lead acetate. When the test tube was shaken, a white precipitate of $PbCl_2$ formed.

   a. Have you increased or decreased the Pb^{+2} concentration by adding lead acetate?

   _____

   b. According to Le Chatelier's Principle, what must happen? _____
   _____
   _____
   _____

   c. Do the observations agree with Le Chatelier's Principle? _____

   d. Explain your answer on the basis of the observations. _____
   _____
   _____
   _____

2.33 The student placed 10 ml of $PbCl_2$ (saturated solution) in a test tube and added a pinch of $NaNO_3$. When the test tube was shook, the $NaNO_3$ dissolved but no precipitate formed. Explain this lack of precipitation by using Le Chatelier's Principle. _____

_____

_____

_____

_____

2.34 The principle that we have investigated here is called the *common ion* effect. Based upon the observations in 2.31 to 2.33, make a general statement as to what is meant by a common ion effect and how this principle is related to equilibrium. _____

_____

_____

_____

_____

2.35 Make a general statement about what conditions are necessary in order to get a precipitate to form in a *saturated solution*. _____

_____

_____

_____

Adult Check _____
               Initial   Date

Problems. All of the ideas you have learned in the preceding activities have direct application. Many problems can be solved by applying the principles of equilibriums, common ion effect, and a saturated solution.

The K_{sp} value is a fixed value for each solubility equilibrium. Every time the same conditions of temperature and pressure are achieved, the same K_{sp} applies. Remember that $K_{sp} = [C]^c [D]^d$ for the general equation $aA + bB \rightleftharpoons cC + dD$. Whenever the calculated $[C]^c [D]^d$ is greater than the K_{sp}, a precipitate will form. The K_{sp} is the saturated level of the system and any value greater than that will cause the precipitate to form.

Do these activities.

2.36 Write the K_{sp} expressions for the following reactions.

a. $BaSO_{4(s)} \rightleftharpoons Ba^{+2}_{(aq)} + SO_4^{-2}_{(aq)}$ $K_{sp} = $ _____

b. $Zn(OH)_{2(s)} \rightleftharpoons Zn^{+2}_{(aq)} + 2 OH^-_{(aq)}$ $K_{sp} = $ _____

c. $Ca_3(PO_4)_{2(s)} \rightleftharpoons 3 Ca^{+2}_{(aq)} + 2 PO_4^{-3}_{(aq)}$ $K_{sp} = $ _____

2.37 Will a precipitate form in the following system? *Show all of your calculations:*

To one liter of 0.001 M H^2SO_4 is added 0.002 mole of solid $Pb(NO_3)_2$.

$K_{sp} = 1.3 \times 10^{-8}$ for $PbSO_4$ $PbSO_{4(s)} \rightleftharpoons Pb^{+2}_{(aq)} + SO_4^{-2}_{(aq)}$

a. As the $Pb(NO_3)_2$ dissolves, will a precipitate form? _____

b. State the proof for your answer.

2.38   Suppose you dilute 10 ml of 1.0 M $AgNO_3$ to one liter with tap water.

a. If the chloride concentration in the tap water is about 10^{-5} M, will a precipitate of AgCl form? _____ (K_{sp} = 1.7 x 10^{-10})

b. Show the proof of your answer.

2.39   *OPTIONAL:* The solubility product at 100°C of AgCl is 2.15 x 10^{-8}. Calculate the number of moles of AgCl dissolved in one liter of solution.

2.40   *OPTIONAL:* Experiments have shown that 0.0059 grams of $SrCO_3$ will dissolve in 1 liter of water at 25°C. What is the K_{sp} of $SrCO_3$?

2.41   *OPTIONAL:* Based upon the K_{sp} values and the Ag^+ necessary for each compound to form a precipitate, explain the observations for the dissolving of the $Ag_2CrO_{4(s)}$ and the forming of the $AgCl_{(s)}$. Use the K_{sp} values shown if needed.

K_{sp} = $[Ag^+]\,[Cl^-]$ = 1.7 x 10^{-10} K_{sp} = $[Ag^+]^2\,[CrO_4^{-2}]$ = 9 x 10^{-12}

DATA TABLE 7

Compound	Temperature	K_{sp}
AgCl	4.7	0.21 x 10^{-10}
AgCl	9.7	0.37 x 10^{-10}
AgCl	25°	1.56 x 10^{-10}
AgCl	50°	13.2 x 10^{-10}
AgCl	100°	215 x 10^{-10}

2.42   Study Data Table 7.

a. From the data table, as the temperature increases does the K_{sp} value increase or decrease?
_____

b. Does this change mean that the AgCl becomes more or less soluble at higher temperature?
_____

c. Propose a reason that would explain the change in K_{sp} with a change in temperature.
_____
_____
_____

DATA TABLE 8

SOLUBILITY OF COMMON INORGANIC COMPOUNDS IN WATER

THESE IONS FORM		(DISSOLVE) SOLUBLE COMPOUNDS SOLUBILITY GREATER THAN 0.1 M	(WILL NOT DISSOLVE) SLIGHTLY SOLUBLE COMPOUNDS SOLUBILITY LESS THAN 0.1 M
Anions		**Cations**	**Cations**
NO_3^-	nitrate	Most cations	None
CH_3COO^-	acetate	Most cations	Ag^+
Cl^- Br^- I^-	chloride bromide iodide	Most cations	Ag^+, Pb^{+2}, Hg_2^{+2}
SO_4^{-2} CrO_4^{-2}	sulfate chromate	Most cations	Ba^{+2}, Sr^{+2}, Pb^{+2}, Ag^+
S^{-2}	sulfide	NH_4^+, Cations of Column 1, and Cations of Column 2	Most other cations
OH^-	hydroxide	Cations of Column 1 and NH_4^+, Ba^{+2}, and Sr^{+2} of Column 2	Most other cations
CO_3^{-2} PO_4^{-3}	carbonate phosphate	NH_4^+ and Cations of Column I except Li^+	Most other cations
Cations		**Anions**	**Anions**
Na^+, KI^+ and other cations of Column I and NH_4^+		Most anions	None
$H^+_{(aq)}$		Most anions	None

2.43 Chemists consider a substance to be soluble if 0.1 mole or more of the compound dissolves per liter at room temperature. This standard was the basis of Data Table 8. Using this table decide whether the following compounds are soluble or have low solubility, writing *sol* or *low* respectively.

a. $Mg(NO_3)_2 =$ _____

b. $MgCl_2$ $=$ _____

c. $MgSO_4$ $=$ _____

d. $Mg(OH)_2 =$ _____

e. $MgCO_3$ $=$ _____

f. $Ca(NO_3)_2 =$ _____

g. $CaCl_2$ $=$ _____

h. $CaSO_4$ $=$ _____

i. $Ca(OH)_2 =$ _____

j. $PbCl_2$ $=$ _____

k. $Sr(NO_3)_2 =$ _____

l. Al_2S_3 $=$ _____

m. H_2S $=$ _____

n. $Sr(OH)_2 =$ _____

o. $Pb(NO_3)_2 =$ _____

2.44 To a solution containing 0.1 M concentration of each of the ions Ag^+, Fe^{+2}, Cu^+, and Ca^{+2} is added a 2 M NaBr solution, giving precipitate A. After filtering, a sulfide (S^{-2}) solution is added to the remaining solution and a black precipitate formed, precipitate B. This second precipitate was removed by filtration and a 2 M sodium carbonate solution was added to the filtrate giving precipitate C. Based upon Data Table 8 and your ideas about difference in solubilities in water, determine the composition of the three precipitates, A, B, and C. Explain your reasoning.

A. =

B. =

C. =

APPLICATION

The concepts of solubility, common ion effect, and chemical equilibrium have great application in our daily lives. The solubility of digested food into the blood, the formation of caves, and the operation of a water softener all use equilibrium concepts. Some simple applications will be studied in this section.

One of the everyday problems we find in our lives is "bathtub ring." What is its source? Why does it appear when we use "hard" water, and not when we use "soft" water? What are the differences between "hard" water and "soft" water? Can all "hard" water be made "soft"? What are some advantages of "soft" water? How can "soft" water be made? The next investigations will help you to answer some of these questions.

Do these investigations.

These supplies are needed:

distilled or rain water

well (tap) water (hard water)

soft water (from a household water softener)

several test tubes

liquid soap (not detergent)

$CaCl_2$ (ice-thawing compound)

NaCl (table salt)

microscope slides, depression

dropper

NH_4OH (household ammonia)

$Mg(OH)_2$ (milk of magnesia)

$Na_2B_4O_7$ (borax)

Na_2CO_3 (washing soda)

$FeCl_3$ (ferric chloride)

KCl (salt substitute)

K_2CO_3

heat source

microscope

graduated cylinder, 10ml

Follow these directions and complete the activities. Put a check in the box when each step is completed.

☐ 1. Place 10 ml of tap water in one test tube, 10 ml of distilled water in a second test tube, and 10 ml of soft water in a third test tube.

☐ 2. Add 3 drops of liquid soap to each test tube and shake them vigorously. Can you tell the difference between "suds" and "scum"?

2.45   Record the suds observations.

a. tap water _____

b. distilled water _____

c. soft water _____

2.46   Make a preliminary guess to explain the suds in each case.

_____

_____

☐ 3. Collect data to support or disprove your preliminary guess. Place 5 drops of each sample of water on each of three depression slides.

☐ 4. Place the depression slides on a warm hot plate to evaporate all the water from the slide.

☐ 5. When the water has completely evaporated from the slides, place them under a microscope and observe any deposits and any differences in the shape of the crystals forming the deposits.

2.47   Record your observations.

a. tap water _____

b. distilled water _____

c. soft water _____

☐ 6. One procedure for determining the effect of various ions on soap sudsing is to use a reverse procedure. This reverse procedure involves adding ions to distilled water in a test tube. Add 3 drops of the salt solution or a pinch of the solid salts to 5 ml of distilled water in separate test tubes.

☐ 7. Add 3 drops of soap to each.

☐ 8. Shake the test tube to produce a sudsing action. Note if suds or scum are produced. Data Table 9 should serve to direct you.

2.48   Record of results.

DATA TABLE 9

Salt Solution	+	-	Suds or Scum
$CaCl_2$ (ice - thawing compound)	Ca	Cl	
$Mg(OH)_2$	Mg	OH	
NaCl (table salt)	Na	Cl	
KCl	K	Cl	
$FeCl_3$	Fe	Cl	
Na_2CO_3	Na	CO_3	
$Na_2B_4O_7$ (borax)	Na	B_4O_7	
K_2CO_3	K	CO_3	
NH_4OH (ammonia)	NH_4	OH	

2.49   Study Data Table 9 carefully. Which solutions produce a scum?
        a. _____   b. _____   c. _____

2.50   From this investigation what conclusion can you draw regarding the ions that are responsible for scum? Give evidence to support your conclusion. _____

        _____

        _____

        _____

2.51   A bottle of $CaCl_2$ and a bottle of NaCl have lost their labels. You must relabel these bottles by identifying them. Explain how a soap solution could be used to solve this problem.

        _____

        _____

        _____

        _____

2.52   Three bottles of water are unlabeled. One is known to contain hard water. Another bottle contains water softened by passing the water through a water softener. Another bottle contains distilled water. Suggest a *specific* test that can be used to identify the three bottles of water.

        _____

        _____

        _____

        _____

        _____

Review the material in this section in preparation for the Self Test. The Self Test will check your mastery of this particular section as well as your knowledge of the previous section.

Use the Periodic Table of Elements that came with Science LIFEPAC 1101 as necessary for this test.

Circle the correct response(s) (each answer, 3 points).

2.01   Circle the members of the following list that are ions. (More than one answer may be correct.)

a. Cu   c. PO_4^{-3} e. HCO_3^- g. Al^{+3}

b. Hg_2^{+2} d. Na_2CO^3 f. Fe   h. Zn

2.02   Which member of each of the following pairs has the greatest conductivity when 0.1 mole is dissolved in 1 liter of water? (Circle one member of each pair.)

a. NaCl or NaF   c. AlF_3 or BaF_2

b. $MgCl_2$ or NaCl   d. $SrCl_2$ or $BaCl_2$

2.03   Electricity is conducted through a solution containing an electrolyte by _____ .

a. ions   c. molecules   e. water

b. atoms   d. neutrons

2.04   The solution most likely to conduct the greatest current is _____ .

a. 0.1 M NaCl   c. 0.1 M $CaCl_2$ e. 0.1 M water

b. 0.1 M KCl   d. 0.1 M $MgCl_2$

2.05   When one mole of sodium chloride dissociates in water it produces _____ .

a. 1 mole of ions   d. $^1/_2$ mole of sodium ions

b. 2 moles of ions   e. none of these

c. $^1/_2$ mole of chloride ions

2.06   Which of the following choices is *not* a factor in the amount of electrical conductivity of a solution?

a. concentration   c. ionic character   e. size of container

b. potential number of ions   d. type of solvent

2.07   A solution of calcium chloride, $CaCl_2$, will lower the freezing point of water to a greater extent than an equal concentration of sodium chloride because the solution of calcium chloride _____ .

a. absorbs more heat   d. is more deliquescent

b. ionizes more completely   e. has a more positive ion, Ca^{+2}

c. produces more ions

2.08   An ion can have all of the following characteristics *except* _____ .

a. that it is made of one or more atoms

b. that it has an equal number of protons and electrons

c. that it can have either a positive or negative charge

d. that it can have a charge of +4

e. in solution the plus ions must balance the minus ions

2.09   As the concentration of a given solution increases, the conductivity of a solution _____ .

a. increases   d. no way to predict

b. remains the same   e. increases then decreases

c. decreases

2.010   A solution of 0.1 M NaCl conducts more electricity than a 0.1 M NaI solution mostly because
_____ .

        a. NaCl has a higher number of potential ions
        b. NaI is less ionic in bond character
        c. the electronegativity of Na changes when combined with I
        d. one mole of NaI weighs more and therefore takes more water to cause it to dissolve
        e. there is no explanation. It just conducts more.

2.011   The gram-formula-weight of $CaCl_2$ is 111.1 g. In order to make up 500 ml of a 0.5 M
solution you need _____ .
        a. 55.6 g   c. 27.8 g   e. 222.2 g
        b. 111.1 g   d. 34.4 g

Complete these statements (each answer, 3 points).

2.012   At the point where a solution is in equilibrium with the dissolved-undissolved state,
the solution is _____ .

2.013   The variables affecting the rate of dissolving are these: a. _____
        b. _____   c. _____ , and
        d. _____

2.014   If a crystal of KNO_3 is added to a saturated solution of KNO_3, the solution will
_____ .

2.015   The K_{sp} expression for the system $PbCl_2 \rightleftharpoons Pb^{+2} + 2\ Cl^-$ is _____ .

Make the following calculations (each answer, 5 points).

2.016   Balance this equation. $AgNO_3 + MgCl_2 \rightleftharpoons AgCl + Mg(NO_3)_2$

2.017   Determine the g.f.w. for $Na_2S_2O_3$. (Na = 23.0; S = 32.0; O = 16.0)

2.018   The K_{sp} for AgI is 1×10^{-16}. When AgI dissociates, the reaction is $AgI \rightleftharpoons Ag^+ + I^-$,
Experiments show that the I^- concentration of saltwater is 1.0×10^{-8} moles per liter. What is
the smallest concentration of Ag^+ that can be used to get a precipitate of AgI?

Score   _____
Adult check   _____
             Initial   Date

III. ACID-BASE EQUILIBRIUMS

Solomon, under the inspiration of the Holy Spirit, wrote in Proverbs 10:26, "As vinegar to the teeth, and as smoke to the eyes, so is the sluggard to them that send him." Anyone that has put a bone in vinegar has found that after about twenty-four hours the bone is very rubbery. The vinegar has reacted with the calcium in the bone and softened it greatly. The same reaction occurs with teeth and vinegar since a tooth is a form of a bone. God is telling us that as vinegar will cause teeth to become worthless, unreliable, and ineffective to the mouth, so a sluggard is worthless, unreliable, and ineffective to his employer. As Christians we have a responsibility in all that we do to be as the strong tooth, not the vinegar-affected tooth.

SECTION OBJECTIVES

Review these objectives. When you have completed this section, you should be able to:

10. Define and identify an acid.
11. Define and identify a base.
12. Describe neutralization.
13. Define and apply pH.
14. Apply equilibrium concepts to acid-base reactions.
15. Define and identify a salt.

ACIDS

Acids are common chemicals in our life. In this section you will study what acids are, how you can identify them, their characteristics, and some common examples.

Definition. What are acids? What are we talking about when we say that we have acid indigestion? We have probably all seen advertisements that show the "drip, drip, drip" of excess stomach acid caused by overeating or excess tension. One commercial states that a certain product neutralizes more acid than all others. What do all these claims mean? You will investigate some of these questions.

You will study some common acids. A few are listed in the following table.

ACID	FORMULA	USES
Acetic	$HC_2H_3O_2$	as a solvent for some organic compounds used in making cellulose acetate and is found in vinegar
Hydrochloric	HCl	for cleaning metals
Hydrofluoric	HF	to etch designs on glass; to refine petroleum
Nitric	HNO_3	in manufacturing fertilizers, explosives, and coated fabrics
Sulfuric	H_2SO_4	in the manufacture of fertilizers, refining of petroleum, production of fabrics and explosives

Look carefully at the formulas. One element is found present in each acid. This element, hydrogen, gives acids their properties.

Acids in general are very dangerous chemicals to work with, but in some cases they are found in the foods we eat. You might describe as sour the taste of such foods as lemons, grapefruit, limes, or vinegar. This sour taste results from the acid in that food.

Since acids are chemicals to handle with care, we surely would not like to have to taste things to determine whether they are acids. Chemists have found another way. They have found that some things change color when put with an acid. These chemicals are called *indicators*. When an acid is put with an indicator the color of the indicator changes. Blue litmus is used very often to test for acids. (Litmus comes from various types of lichens.) When blue litmus comes in contact with an acid, the litmus turns from blue to red.

Another characteristic of acids is that they react with metals to produce hydrogen. A typical reaction is $Mg + 2\,HCl \longrightarrow MgCl_2 + H_2\uparrow$. This type of reaction is called an oxidation-reduction reaction, and you will study how it works in Section IV of this LIFEPAC.

Acids react with water to ionize and form the hydronium ion, H_3O^+. An example is $H_2S + H_2O \rightleftharpoons H_3O^+ + HS^-$. No separate H^+ can exist very long without attaching to some other ion or molecule. In a water solution the polar water molecule is an ideal acceptor of the positive ion. The H_3O^+ ion geometry is similar to the NH_3 molecule, polar-pyramidal in shape.

K_a. The equilibrium expression for acids is K_a. A typical acid ionizes in this way: $HB \rightleftharpoons H^+ + B^-$. Then $K_a = \dfrac{[H^+]\,[B^-]}{HB}$. As the K_a increases, the concentration of H^+ and B^- increases also. Study Data Table 10.

DATA TABLE 10

RELATIVE STRENGTHS OF ACIDS IN AQUEOUS SOLUTION AT ROOM TEMPERATURE

All ions are equated.

$$HB \rightleftharpoons H^+_{(aq)} + B^-_{(aq)} \qquad\qquad K_a = \frac{[H^+]\,[B^-]}{[HB]}$$

Acid	Strength	Reaction	K_a
hydroiodic acid	very strong	$HI \rightleftharpoons H^+ + I^-$	very large
hydrobromic acid		$HBr \rightleftharpoons H^+ + Br^-$	very large
hydrochloric acid		$HCl \rightleftharpoons H^+ + Cl^-$	very large
nitric acid		$HNO_3 \rightleftharpoons H^+ + NO_3^-$	very large
sulfuric acid		$H_2SO_4 \rightleftharpoons H^+ + HSO_4$	large
hydrated hydrogen ion		$H_3O^+ \rightleftharpoons H^+ + H_2O$	1.0
oxalic acid	strong	$HOOCCOOH \rightleftharpoons H^+ + HOOCCOO^-$	5.4×10^{-2}
sulfurous acid ($SO_2 + H_2O$)		$H_2SO_3 \rightleftharpoons H^+ + HSO_3^-$	1.7×10^{-2}
hydrogen sulfate ion		$HSO_4^- \rightleftharpoons H^+ + SO_4^{2-}$	1.3×10^{-2}
phosphoric acid		$H_3PO_4 \rightleftharpoons H^+ + H_2PO_4^-$	7.1×10^{-3}
hydrofluoric acid	weak	$HF \rightleftharpoons H^+ + F^-$	6.7×10^{-4}
nitrous acid		$HNO_2 \rightleftharpoons H^+ + NO_2^-$	5.1×10^{-4}
benzoic acid		$C_6H_5COOH \rightleftharpoons H^+ + C_6H_5COO^-$	6.6×10^{-5}
hydrogen oxalate ion		$HOOCCOO^- \rightleftharpoons H^+ + OOCCOO^{2-}$	5.4×10^{-5}
acetic acid	weak	$CH_3COOH \rightleftharpoons H^+ + CH_3COO^-$	1.8×10^{-5}
carbonic acid ($CO_2 + H_2O$)		$H_2CO_3 \rightleftharpoons H^+ + HCO_3^-$	4.4×10^{-7}
hydrogen sulfide		$H_2S \rightleftharpoons H^+ + HS^-$	1.0×10^{-7}
dihydrogen phosphate ion		$H_2PO_4^- \rightleftharpoons H^+ + HPO_4^{2-}$	6.3×10^{-8}
hydrogen sulfite ion		$HSO_3^- \rightleftharpoons H^+ + SO_3^{2-}$	6.2×10^{-8}
ammonium ion	weak	$NH_4^+ \rightleftharpoons H^+ + NH_3$	5.7×10^{-10}
hydrogen carbonate ion		$HCO_3^- \rightleftharpoons H^+ + CO_3^{2-}$	$4\,7 \times 10^{-11}$
hydrogen peroxide	very weak	$H_2O_2 \rightleftharpoons H^+ + HO_2^-$	2.4×10^{-12}
monohydrogen phosphate ion		$HPO_4^{2-} \rightleftharpoons H^+ + PO_4^{3-}$	4.4×10^{-13}
hydrogen sulfide ion		$HS^- \rightleftharpoons H^+ + S^{2-}$	1.3×10^{-13}
water		$H_2O \rightleftharpoons H^+ + OH^-$	1.8×10^{-16}*
hydroxide ion		$OH^- \rightleftharpoons H^+ + O^{2-}$	$< 10^{-36}$
ammonia	very weak	$NH_3 \rightleftharpoons H^+ + NH_2^-$	very small

* $K_w = K_A(55.5) = 1 \times 10^{-14}$

Do these activities.

3.1 Draw an enthalpy diagram for the following equilibrium systems.

a. $HCl \rightleftharpoons H + Cl^-$ b. $H_2S \rightleftharpoons H^+ + HS^-$

3.2 When the K_a value is very large, the a. _____ are favored over the b. _____ .

3.3 Notice that the second H^+ is more difficult to remove from any substance than the first. For example, the K_a of $H_2S \rightleftharpoons H^+ + HS^-$ is greater than the K_a of $HS^- \rightleftharpoons H^+ + S^{-2}$. Explain why this difference occurs. (Hint: Remember the HS^- is already negative.)

_____

_____

_____

_____

_____

_____

 Answer *true* **or** *false.*

3.4 _____ A large K_a favors the product side of the equilibrium.

3.5 _____ Litmus is a strong acid.

3.6 _____ A large K_a means a strong acid.

3.7 _____ Water has a large K_a value.

3.8 _____ Ammonia is a strong acid.

3.9 _____ The greater the H^+ the stronger the acid.

3.10 _____ Sourness of a taste is due to the acid in the food.

Do this investigation.

> **These supplies are needed:**
> distilled water
> 0.1 M HCl (8.3 ml of concentrated HCl per 1 L of solution)
> 0.001 M HCl (1 ml 0.1 M HCl per 100 ml of solution)
> 0.00001 M HCl (1 ml 0.001 M HCl per 100 ml of solution)
> marble, limestone, or chalk chips
> 4 test tubes

SCIENCE

1 1 0 7

LIFEPAC TEST

68 / 85

Name _____

Date _____

Score _____

SCIENCE 1107: LIFEPAC TEST

Answer *true* **or** *false* (each answer, 1 point).

1. _____ The substance NO_3^- is an ion.
2. _____ The substance CCl_4 is a molecule.
3. _____ A saturated solution is not at equilibrium.
4. _____ The solution 1 M H_2SO_4 conducts more current than 1 M HCl.
5. _____ An acid is bitter and brackish.

Choose the best response (each answer, 3 points).

6. As the solution of 100 ml of 1.00 M HNO_3 is mixed with 100 ml of 0.100 M KOH, what is the resulting $[H^+]$ after the reaction is finished?

   a. 0.900 M   c. 9.00 M   e. neither a, b, c, nor d

   b. 0.500 ml   d. 0.450 M

7. The weak acid $HC_2H_3O_2$ has an equilibrium expression of $K_{eq} = \dfrac{[H^+][C_2H_3O_2^-]}{[HC_2H_3O_2]}$

   The $K_{eq} = 1.8 \times 10^{-5}$. If the $[HC_2H_3O_2] = 0.10$ M, what is the $[H^+]$?

   a. 1.34×10^{-3} c. 1.8×10^{-4} e. 4.2×10^{-3}

   b. 3.6×10^{-4} d. 1×10^{-2}

8. An acid is _____ .

   a. a proton acceptor

   b. any compound with hydrogen as a cation

   c. any compound containing hydrogen

   d. a proton donor

   e. a compound having hydrogen as a cation and oxygen as an anion.

9. What causes a solution to conduct or not to conduct electricity?

   a. Presence or absence of ions.

   b. Presence or absence of electrons.

   c. Presence or absence of a metal.

   d. Presence or absence of protons.

10. Electrolytes are defined as those compounds which _____ .

   a. have covalent bonding

   b. produce less lowering at the freezing point than do compounds like sugar

   c. have only ionic bonds

   d. dissolve in a solvent such as water to produce a solution which conducts electric current easily

11. How many milliliters of 0.02 M HCl are needed to react completely with 100 ml of 0.01 M NaOH?

    a. 100 ml   c. 50 ml   e. 75 ml

    b. 200 ml   d. 25 ml

The solubility product constants for some silver salts at room temperature are given.

Salts	K_{sp}
$AgCH_3COO$	2×10^{-3}
$AgIO_3$	3×10^{-8}
$AgCl$	1×10^{-10}
$AgBr$	1×10^{-14}
AgI	1×10^{-16}

12. Ten milliliters each of 0.1 M solutions of $NaCH_3COO$, $NaIO_2$, $NaCl$, $NaBr$, and NaI are placed in a small beaker and thoroughly mixed. One drop of 0.01 M $AgNO_3$ is added to the mixture. A precipitate of only one of the anions remains after equilibrium is reached. The precipitate is most likely to b.

    a. $AgCH_3COO$ c. $AgCl$ e. AgI

    b. $AgIO_3$ d. $AgBr$

13. A solution with a pH of 8.5 is said to be _____ .

    a. strongly basic   c. strongly acidic   e. neutral

    b. slightly basic   d. slightly acidic

14. The g.f.w. of $Ca(OH)_2$ is _____ . (Ca = 40.; O = 16.; H = 1.)

    a. 57 g   c. 74 g   e. 97 g

    b. 58 g   d. 114 g

15. The sum of the pH and pOH is _____ .

    a. 0   c. -7   e. 14

    b. 7   d. 10

Complete these statements (each answer, 3 points).

16. The factors that affect the rate of dissolving of a solute are a. _____ ,

    b. _____ , c. _____ , and d. _____ .

17. A salt is defined as _____

    _____ .

18. The three main characteristics of a solution are its a. _____ ,

    b. _____ , and c. _____ .

19. In the reaction $Zn^0 + Cu^{+2} \rightleftharpoons Zn^{+2} + Cu^0$ the oxidizing agent is the _____ .

20. A reducing agent _____ electrons.

Do these calculations (each answer 5 points).

21. Determine the oxidation numbers for the atom that is underlined in each of the following compounds.

    a. HO$\underline{Cl}$ _____

    b. $\underline{N}_2H_4$ _____

    c. Na$_2\underline{O}_2$ _____

22. Complete the following equation. Determine the net voltage of the cell and decide whether a reaction will occur.

    $$Sn + Fe^{+2} \longrightarrow$$

NOTES

Follow these directions and complete the activities. Put a check in the box when each step is completed.

- ❏ 1. Set up four test tubes in a rack.
- ❏ 2. Add a small marble chip to each of the test tubes.
- ❏ 3. Add acid solutions as labeled in the chart.
- ❏ 4. Observe whether reaction takes place and how fast. Record your results.
- ❏ 5. Pour the acid solution from each test tube into the sink.
- ❏ 6. Rinse the marble chips with water and place them in a container for this purpose to be used again.

3.11   Record the results.

ACID STRENGTH	REACTION	HOW FAST?
.1 M HCl		
.001 M HCl		
.00001 M HCl		
.0000001 HCl (distilled H_2O or neutral water)		

3.12   Marble is made from limestone under the influence of heat and pressure. The chemical formula for limestone or marble chips is $CaCO_3$. When you added the chips to the acid solutions, they effervesce (bubble or foam).

a. What is the gas that is produced?   _____

b. What is the chemical formula of the gas?   _____

c. How could you test rocks for the presence of limestone?

_____

_____

d. Write a balanced symbol model for the reaction of limestone with hydrochloric acid.

- -

3.13   *OPTIONAL:* An extension might be the testing of samples of rock for the presence of limestone or calcium carbonate. This identification could be done by completing a chart similar to the following one. You will require some outside reading to identify and name the samples used for testing. Get some rock samples from your area, list, and identify them.

Sample	Does it react with HCl?	Description (color, hardness, texture)	Type	Name
1				
2				
3				
4				
5				
6				
7				

Adult Check _____

Initial   Date

BASES

Bases are the next category of chemicals that you will study. This group of chemicals all have very similar properties and are common to your everyday life. Lye, NaOH, and ammonia, NH_4OH, are two examples.

Definition. Bases are opposite to acids. Acids are hydrogen (proton, H^+) donors, and bases are hydrogen acceptors. Most common bases are hydroxides (that is, they contain OH^-). Some common examples are listed in the following table.

Chemical Name	Common Name	Formula	Uses
Ammonium hydroxide	Aqua ammonia	NH_4OH	in household cleaning
Calcium hydroxide	Limewater (slaked lime)	$Ca(OH)_2$	in whitewash and mortar
Magnesium hydroxide	Hydrated magnesia (milk of magnesia)	$Mg(OH)_2$	as a laxative and to neutralize excess acid in the stomach (a constituent of milk of magnesia)
Potassium hydroxide	Caustic potash	KOH	in making soft soap
Sodium hydroxide	Caustic soda (lye)	$NaOH$	in cleaning and in soap-making

Bases also have a bitter, flat, or brackish taste. The "bad" taste of soap comes from the base that is used in its manufacture. Bases have a very soapy feel and are slippery to the touch.

Bases react with red litmus paper and turn it blue. This reaction with litmus is opposite to that of acids.

K$_b$. Bases have an equilibrium expression just as acids do. K$_b$ values are reciprocal values to the K$_a$ values. This relationship means that strong acids are weak bases and that weak acids are strong bases. The greater the K$_a$, the smaller the K$_b$.

$$HB \rightleftharpoons H^+ + B \quad H^+ + B^- \rightleftharpoons HB$$

$$K_a = \frac{[H^+][B]}{[HB]} \qquad K_b = \frac{[HB]}{[H^+][B]}$$

The K$_b$ for $H^+ + HS^- \rightleftharpoons H_2S$ equals $1/_{1 \times 10^{-7}}$, which is $1/_{K_a}$.

Do these activities.

3.14   According to Data Table 10 (page 34), what is the strongest base? _____

3.15   Look at Data Table 10. What is the weakest base? _____

3.16   List three characteristics of a base.

   a. _____

   b. _____

   c. _____

3.17   What is the most common ion present in a base? _____

3.18   Describe the relationship between K$_a$ and K$_b$. _____

_____

_____

_____

_____

---

pH SCALE

Frequently a chemist wishes to know whether a substance is acidic or basic. Many advertisements stress that a product is pH balanced, pH controlled, or pH adjusted. What is pH? How is pH important? Why are pH values important to us in our everyday life?

Definition. Acid solutions owe their acidity to the hydrogen ions (H$^+$) which they contain. The more hydrogen ions that are in a given volume of solution, the more strongly acidic is the solution. Alkaline, or basic, solutions, owe their alkalinity to hydroxide ions (OH$^-$). In a neutral solution equal (and very small) amounts of these two kinds of ions are present.

The pH system is a method of stating the acidity or alkalinity of a solution. For many purposes stating the pH value is more convenient than stating the actual quantity of hydrogen or hydroxide ions. The pH value is based upon the negative logarithm of the hydrogen ion concentration. To use pH in a simple way, you only need to know that a neutral solution has a pH of 7; that the lower the pH goes below 7, the more acidic the solution is; and that the higher it goes above 7, the more alkaline is the solution.

The chart shows that the pH of pure water is 7; that is, it is neutral. The pH of the two hydrochloric acid solutions shown on the scale is low, and as you would expect, the 1 M solution has a lower pH than the 0.1 M because it is more strongly acidic. Since acetic acid is a weaker acid than hydrochloric acid, its solutions, though still below 7 in pH, are higher on the scale than those of hydrochloric acid.

Common chemicals	Common substances	pH	Concentration of H$^+$ ions in moles per liter at 25° C	
1 M Hydrochloric acid		0		
1 M Sulfuric acid				
0.1 M Hydrochloric acid		1	0.1	(10^{-1})
0.1 M Sulfuric acid	Limes			
	Lemons	2	.01	(10^{-2})
1 M Acetic acid				
0.1 M Acetic acid				
	Apples	3	.001	(10^{-3})
Carbonic acid (sat.)				
	Tomatoes	4	.0001	(10^{-4})
	Bananas			
0.1 M Boric acid		5	.00001	(10^{-5})
	Bread			
	Peas	6	.000001	(10^{-6})
	Cow's Milk			
Water (pure)		7	.0000001	(10^{-7})
	Blood Plasma			
	Eggs, fresh white	8	.00000001	(10^{-8})
0.1 M Sodium bicarbonate				
	Seawater			
		9	.000000001	(10^{-9})
Ferrous hydroxide (sat.)				
		10	.0000000001	(10^{-10})
	Milk of Magnesia			
0.1 M Ammonia		11	.00000000001	(10^{-11})
1 M Ammonia				
		12	.000000000001	(10^{-12})
0.1 M Sodium hydroxide				
		13	.0000000000001	(10^{-13})
1 M Sodium hydroxide		14	.00000000000001	(10^{-14})

ACIDIC

NEUTRAL

BASIC

Near the bottom of the scale we find a sodium hydroxide solution. Sodium hydroxide is a strong base; hence, its solution is strongly alkaline. Ammonium hydroxide is a weaker base; therefore, the pH of its solution is lower.

Applications of pH. Many chemical reactions are influenced by the pH of the solution in which they occur. For example, in qualitative analysis, chemists frequently pass hydrogen sulfide gas through a solution of metallic salts to cause the precipitation of the sulfides of the metals. Certain sulfides such as copper sulfide will precipitate at any pH, however low; but others, such as zinc sulfide, precipitate only when the pH is above a certain value. Thus, if the chemist wishes to precipitate the sulfide of one metal but to leave another in solution, he must know the pH values required and be able to adjust the pH of the solution to correspond. A similar situation arises in dozens of the operations of analytical chemistry.

In industrial chemistry the control of the pH of a solution is often necessary to promote the desired reactions. For example, in the process by which bromine is obtained from sea water, the pH of the seawater must first be lowered from its normal value of 7.2 to a value between 3 and 4. This process is done by adding sulfuric acid. Similar adjustments of pH are often made in the clarification, disinfection, and softening of water supplies.

Biologists and physicians make constant use of pH values. The pH of blood, as shown on the chart, normally lies between 7.3 and 7.5. If the pH goes much below 7.0 or above 7.8 death results. Bacteriologists have found that each kind of bacteria grows best at a particular pH, and the same is true of the various kinds of yeasts and molds that bring about fermentations.

Even the farmer is interested in pH values because the size of his crops depends upon the pH of the soil being suitable for the particular kind of plant he is raising. For example, sugar beets do best if the pH of the soil lies between 7.0 and 7.5, whereas cranberries thrive if the pH is as low as 4 or 5.

 Do these activities.

3.19   Analyze this diagram.

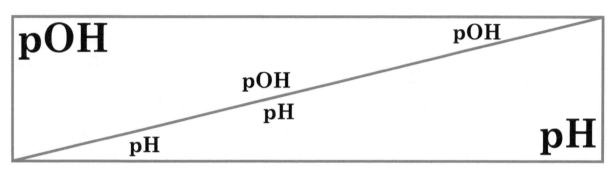

$[H^+] = 1 \times 10^0$	$\longleftarrow$		1×10^{-7}	$\longrightarrow$	1×10^{-14}
$[OH^-] = 1 \times 10^{-14}$		Acidic	1×10^{-7}	Basic	1×10^0
pH = 0			7		14
pOH = 14			7		0

a. Using the diagram as a reference, what is the pH when a solution has a $[H^+] = 1$?
   pH = _____

b. A neutral solution has a pH = _____

c. When a solution is basic, the pH is greater than _____ .

d. What relationship do you find between the pH number and the power of 10 used to express the $[H^+]$? _____

_____

_____

e. Does a similar relationship exist between the pOH and $[OH^-]$? _____

f. What is true about the sum of the (pH + pOH) for each concentration?

_____

_____

_____

3.20 Complete the following chart based upon the ideas of pH and pOH.

Increasing Acidity →

[H₃O⁺]	[OH]	pH	pOH
10^1			
10^0			
	10^{-13}		
10^{-2}			
	10^{-11}		
		4	
	10^{-9}		
10^{-5}			
		7	
	10^{-6}		
			5
	10^{-4}		
10^{-11}			
	10^{-2}		
		13	
10^{-14}			
			-1

↓ Increasing Basicity

How to Calculate pH from the [H₃O⁺]:

In 1909 Sorensen devised a way to calculate pH from the log of the hydrogen ion concentration.

$$pH = 1/[H_3O^+] \text{ or } pH = -\log [H_3O^+]$$

With our calculators it is a simple matter to find the log of any number.

Once you have changed the [H⁺] to scientific notation you must locate the log button on your calculator. Some calculators require you to push log before you enter the value most require it after.

To find the –log:

Ex. pH = –log [3.4 x 10⁻⁸]

    1.   Key in 3.4
    2.   Press the Exp button (or the EE button)*
    3.   Key in 8 for the exponent
    4.   Press the +/– button to make the exponent negative
    5.   Press the log button
    6.   Press the +/– button to find the –log.
    7.   This should yield an answer of 7.5.**

*If you have a graphing calculator or a more advanced scientific your EE button might be a second level function, you will look above your buttons at the yellow symbols and locate EE. You will have to push 2ⁿᵈ EE to get an exponent.

**If this technique does not work or you get an error message do the above steps but move steps 5 and 6 to the beginning.

Many times you will be given a pH and asked to find the hydrogen ion concentration. This is called finding the antilog. With a calculator this is an easy problem. All scientific calculators that have a log button will also have a shift or second function button. This button often reverses the function of whatever you push.

To find the antilog:

    1.   Key in your pH
    2.   Press the +/– button to make it negative
    3.   Press the shift or 2ⁿᵈ function button
    4.   Press the log button
    5.   The number you see is the [H⁺]

You can use these same steps to convert your [OH⁻] to pOH.

We will outline the basic steps without a calculator here so that you might have a deeper understanding.

If you have a solution whose [H⁺] is 10⁻⁵ moles/liter, we must change that to scientific notation:

$$[H^+] = 1 \times 10^{-5}$$

The "1" is referred to as the mantissa and exponent is called the characteristic. To determine pH from this number we must take the –log. When we use the rules of logarithms we see this expands to:

$$pH = -\log (1 \times 10^{-5}) = - (\log 1 + \log (10^{-5}))$$

The log of 1 is always 0 and the log of the power of ten is the exponent.

We add these together and get: pH = –(0 + (–5)) = 5

This is very easy if the mantissa is "1" but if it is not we use the same strategy but we must find the log of the mantissa which would require a log table or a calculator.

- -

3.21   *OPTIONAL:* The values used in the scale of pH and pOH are derived from a system designed by Sorensen in 1909. His system allows for the elimination of a very awkward set of calculations involving the strengths of acid and base solutions, which use negative exponents. Sorensen's system is based upon logarithms. (Logarithm tables are needed for the calculations.)

pH = $\log \frac{1}{[H_3O^+]}$; or pH = 1 log $[H_3O^+]$. For example, if the $[H^+]$ = 10^{-5}

moles/liter then: pH = $\log \frac{1}{[H^+]}$ = $\log \frac{1}{10^{-5}}$ = 5 log 10 = 5

Suppose, however, that the $[H^+]$ = 4×10^{-3} moles/liter.

Then, pH = $\log \frac{1}{[H^+]}$ = $\log \frac{1}{4 \times 10^{-3}}$ = $\log \frac{10^3}{4}$ = $\log 10^3$ - log 4 = 3 - 0.60 = <u>2.40</u>

a. What would be if the pH of the $[H^+]$ = 3×10^{-5} moles/liter?
    Show your work.

b. What would be the pOH of the above solution? _____

c. If a solution had an $[OH^-]$ = 3×10^{-10} moles/liter, what would be the pH value of this solution? *Show your calculations.*

d. If the pH value was 3.6, what is the $[H^+]$? *Show your work.*

42

3.22   The pH of a solution can be determined with an instrument called a pH meter. The following data was collected with the use of a pH meter. Study and analyze it carefully.

	Solution	pH reading	Acid or Base?
(Hydrochloric acid)	0.1 M HCl	0.1	_____
	0.01 M HCl	1.1	_____
(Sodium carbonate)	0.1 M Na_2CO_3	10.3	_____
(Sodium hydroxide)	0.1 M NaOH	13.0	_____
(Acetic acid)	0.1 M $HC_2H_3O_2$	2.8	_____
	0.01 M $HC_2H_3O_2$	3.6	_____
(Sodium bicarbonate)	0.1 M $NaHCO_3$	8.2	_____

a. Complete the last column of the preceding data table.

b. What caused the different pH values for the test solutions?
_____

c. Why does the NaOH solution have a pH when it does not provide any H^+?
_____
_____

d. How might you explain the difference between the pH values of the 0.01 M HCl and the 0.01 M $HC_2H_3O_2$? _____
_____
_____

e. Compare the pH of Na_2CO_3 and $NaHCO_3$. Do you find any difference? _____

f. If so, explain this difference. _____
_____
_____
_____

3.23   List at least three applications of the concept of pH.

a. _____

b. _____

c. _____

NEUTRALIZATION

One of the most important reactions in chemistry, especially in living things, is the reaction between acids and bases. This reaction is called *neutralization*. An example is:

$$Na^+ + OH^- + H^+ + Cl^- \rightleftharpoons Na^+ + Cl^- + H_2O$$

The net reaction involved only the ions that entered into the reaction. Ions that do not participate in the reaction are called *spectator ions*. The net reaction is $H^+ + OH^- \rightleftharpoons H_2O$ with the Na^+ and Cl^- acting as the spectator ions.

Kw. In the reaction $H_2O_{(l)} \rightleftharpoons H^+_{(aq)} + OH^-_{(aq)}$ the concentration of H_2O remains constant in the same way the concentration of a solid $\rightleftharpoons$ dissolved state remained constant. The K_{eq} for $H_2O_{(l)} \rightleftharpoons H^+_{(aq)} + OH^-_{(aq)}$ equals $K_{eq} = \frac{[H^+][OH^-]}{H_2O} = \frac{[H^+][OH^-]}{k_1}$ (k_1 = constant number of 55.5). Therefore, $K_{eq} \cdot k_1 = [H^+][OH^-] = K_W$.

> *The K_W is called the ion product of water.*
> *This value at 25°C is 1.00×10^{-14} in pure water. Each molecule breaks up to form one $OH^-_{(aq)}$ ion and one $H^+_{(aq)}$ ion. This means that for pure water $H^+ = OH^-$.*
> *From the K_W relationship:*

$$K_W = [H^+][OH^-] = [H^+]^2 = 1.00 \times 10^{-14}$$

$$H^+ = [OH^-] = \sqrt{1.00 \times 10^{-14}}$$
$$= 1.00 \times 10^{-7}$$

One might represent Kw graphically:

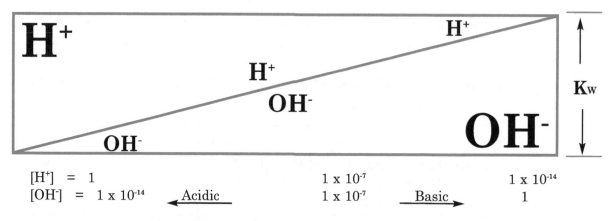

$[H^+] = 1$	1×10^{-7}	1×10^{-14}
$[OH^-] = 1 \times 10^{-14}$ ← Acidic	1×10^{-7} Basic →	1

If a solution is acidic: $[H^+] > [OH^-]$; basic: $[H^+] < [OH^-]$; neutral: $[H^+] = [OH^-]$

 Do these activities.

3.24   Look carefully at the Kw expression.

a. If the $[H^+]$ changed from 10^{-7} to 10^{-4}, will the $[OH^-]$ increase, decrease, or remain the same?

   _____

b. Explain.

   _____

   _____

c. What is the new $[OH^-]$? _____

- -

3.25   *OPTIONAL:* If you made up a solution of NaOH by adding 0.010 mole of solid NaOH to 1.0 liter of distilled water,

a. What would be the concentration of the $OH^-_{(aq)}$?

b. What would be the $[H^+]$ of the solution?

3.26   *OPTIONAL:* Consider this system.

$$CH_3COOH_{(aq)} \rightleftharpoons H^+_{(aq)} + CH_3COO^-_{(aq)} \qquad K_{eq} = 1.8 \times 10^{-5}$$

    a. What will happen to the equilibrium as OH⁻ ions are added? _____

    b. Explain your answer in a.

    _____

    _____

    _____

    _____

    c. One mole of CH_3COOH will require how many moles of OH⁻ for neutralization?

    _____

    d. Explain your answer in c.

    _____

    _____

    _____

3.27   *OPTIONAL:* Concentrated HCl is purchased from a chemical company in a concentration of 11.7 M. Determine the $[H^+]$ and $[OH^-]$ of this water solution of HCl.

3.28   *OPTIONAL:* At 20°C, 0.009 g of $Mg(OH)_2$ is found to saturate one liter of solution. $Mg(OH)_{2(s)} \rightleftharpoons Mg^{+2}_{(aq)} + 2\,OH^-_{(aq)}$. Determine a. the K_{sp} value, b. whether $Mg(OH)_2$ would produce a strongly or weakly conducting water solution, and c. the $[OH^-]$.

    a.

    b.

    c.

Titration. The process of reacting a base with an acid was called neutralization. When the condition of $[H^+]$ = $[OH^-]$ is reached, this state is called the *equivalence point*. The value of the $[H^+]$ at the equivalence point is 10^{-7}. The value of the $[OH^-]$ at the equivalence point is 10^{-7}.

The method that is most often used to find the equivalence point of an acid-base system is called *titration*. Titration is a method by which quantitative amounts of acid or base of known concentration are reacted with a known amount of the other type of solution until the equivalence point is reached. That is, the amount of H^+ used must be equal to the amount of OH^- used. H^+ used = OH^- used. This concept can be represented:

> *(ml H⁺ used) (concentration)* = *(ml OH⁻ used) (concentration)*

The concentration term on each side of the equal sign until now has been expressed as molarity, M; but this way of expressing concentration when titrating is very limited. Solutions of 1 M HCl and H_2SO_4 have the same molar concentration. However, look at the formulas of these two acids carefully. Remembering that acids donate hydrogen ions (protons), one mole of H^+ will be furnished by one mole of HCl; and two moles of H^+ will be furnished by one mole of H_2SO_4.

This fact means that equal molar solutions of H_2SO_4 and HCl will allow for the H_2SO_4 solution to donate twice as many H^+ as the HCl. In a similar manner, 1 M $Ba(OH)_2$ will accept twice as many H^+ as 1 M NaOH. How many times more H^+ will be donated by 1 M H_3PO_4 than by a 1 M HCl solution? (*three*) How many times more H^+ will be accepted by a 1 M $Al(OH)_3$ solution than by 1 M NaOH? (*three*)

The problem in acid-base titrations is to make solutions containing a certain number of moles of H^+ despite the fact that some acids furnish more than a mole of H^+ for each mole of acid dissolved.

The answer is to measure out enough acid to produce just the number of moles of H^+ needed and then dividing by the number of H^+ furnished per molecule.

Example: H_2SO_4 - 1 mole gives 2 moles of H^+ when dissolved.

Therefore, $^1/_2$ mole of H_2SO_4 is needed to create 1 mole of H^+.

When 1 mole of H^+ is created per liter from a certain amount of acid, that solution is said to be a one *normal* solution. To determine a normal value, the following formula can be used:

> number of H^+ per molecule of acid x moles of acid used = normal value

The same reasoning follows for the normality of bases. Normality of bases is determined in this manner:

> number of H^+ accepted per molecule x moles of base used = normal value

Our titration equation can now be more meaningfully written for *all* acid and base concentrations:

> *(ml H⁺ used) (normality)* = *(ml OH⁻ used) (normality)*

 Complete these activities.

3.29   Complete the following table.

Acid	M	N
HCl	1	a. _____
H_2SO_4	1	b. _____
H_3PO_4	1	c. _____
H_2SO_4	.5	d. _____
H_3PO_4	e. _____	.3
KH_2PO_4	f. _____	.2
HNO_3	g. _____	1

Base	M	N
NaOH	h. _____	1
$Ca(OH)_2$	1	i. _____
KOH	1	j. _____
$Ba(OH)_2$	k. _____	1
$Al(OH)_3$	.3	l. _____
NH_3	m. _____	1

3.30   A titration was performed in a lab situation. Instead of the HCl, however, H_2SO_4 was used. The following data was collected:

   ml NaOH = 43.2 ml

   concentration NaOH = 0.15 N

   ml H_2SO_4 = 20.5 ml

a. What is the normality of the H_2SO_4? _____

b. What is the molarity? _____

 Adult Check _____

                      Initial   Date

Salts. Salts are the products of neutralization. When HCl reacts with NaOH and the resulting solution is evaporated to dryness, a solid crystallizes. This solid is sodium chloride, common table salt, NaCl. This salt is a member of a large class of compounds called *salts*. The reaction of an acid and a base produces water and this salt. A general reaction for neutralization can be written:

$$Acid + Base \rightleftharpoons Salt + Water$$

Some specific examples of neutralization reactions are listed.

2 HCl Hydrochloric acid	+	Ca(OH)$_2$ calcium hydroxide	$\longrightarrow$	CaCl$_2$ calcium chloride	+	H$_2$O water
HNO$_3$ Nitric acid	+	NaOH sodium hydroxide	$\longrightarrow$	NaNO$_3$ sodium nitrate	+	H$_2$O water
H$_2$SO$_4$ Sulfuric acid	+	2 NaOH sodium hydroxide	$\longrightarrow$	Na$_2$SO$_4$ sodium sulfate	+	2 H$_2$O water
H$_2$SO$_4$ Sulfuric acid	+	Mg(OH)$_2$ magnesium hydroxide	$\longrightarrow$	MgSO$_4$ magnesium sulfate	+	2 H$_2$O water

Some common salts and their uses are listed:

Name	Formula	Use
Sodium chloride	NaCl	Common table salt. Used in the preparation of sodium compounds.
Copper sulfate	CuSO$_4$	Used in copper plating and fungicides.
Ammonium sulfate	(NH$_4$)$_2$SO$_4$	Used in fertilizer.
Sodium nitrate	NaNO$_3$	Used in fertilizers and in the manufacture of explosives.
Sodium carbonate	Na$_2$CO$_3$	Washing soda. Used in softening water and soap manufacture.
Magnesium sulfate	MgSO$_4$	Laxative, Epsom salts.

47

Do these activities.

3.31   What is a salt? _____

_____

3.32   What is the general equation for neutralization? _____

_____

 Match these items. The answers can be used more than once.

3.33   _____ NH_4Cl a. acid
3.34   _____   HCl   b. base
3.35   _____ H_2SO_4 c. salt
3.36   _____   NaOH
3.37   _____ Na_3PO_4
3.38   _____ H_2NaPO_4
3.39   _____ NH_4OH
3.40   _____   NaCl

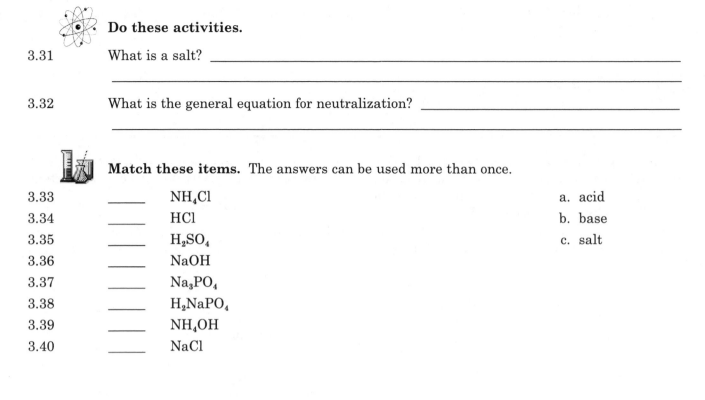 **Adult Check** _____
                        Initial   Date

Review the material in this section in preparation for the Self Test. The Self Test will check your mastery of this particular section as well as your knowledge of previous sections.

Answer *true* **or** *false* (each answer, 1 point).

3.01 _____ Ions are charged atoms or groups of atoms.

3.02 _____ Ionic solutions are poor conductors of electricity.

3.03 _____ Molarity is represented by the symbol m.

3.04 _____ Balanced equations illustrate Conservation of Mass.

3.05 _____ A solution is a homogeneous mixture.

3.06 _____ Polar substances are good solvents for polar solutions.

3.07 _____ Molarity is the same as normality.

3.08 _____ Normality only applies to acids.

3.09 _____ A change in concentration by adding H_2O changes the moles of solute present.

3.010 _____ Titration is a process of reacting an acid with a base until an equivalence point is reached.

Match these items (each answer, 2 points).

3.011 _____ mole weight

3.012 _____ base equilibrium constant

3.013 _____ moles of H^+ per liter of solution

3.014 _____ moles per liter of solution

3.015 _____ spreading out

3.016 _____ substance being dissolved

3.017 _____ general equilibrium constant

3.018 _____ acid equilibrium constant

3.019 _____ the process of breaking from the crystal

3.020 _____ solubility product constant

a. diffusion
b. solute
c. dissolving
d. solvent
e. K_a
f. K_{eq}
g. K_b
h. K_{sp}
i. molarity
j. normality
k. g.f.w.

Choose the correct answer (each answer, 3 points).

3.021 An acid is _____ .

a. a proton acceptor

b. any compound with hydrogen as a cation

c. any compound containing hydrogen

d. a proton donor

e. a compound having hydrogen as a cation and oxygen as an anion.

3.022 A 1 N solution of H_3PO_4 contains how many grams of H_3PO_4 per liter of solution?
(g.f.w. = 98 g)

a. 32.6 g   d. 196 g

b. 49 g   e. 294 g

c. 98 g

3.023 What volume of 0.1 N $Ca(OH)_2$ is required to neutralize 30 ml of 0.1 M HCl?

a. 15 ml   d. 45 ml

b. 30 ml   e. 10 ml

c. 60 ml

3.024   A solution that is neutral has a pH of _____ .

        a. 1   d. 14

        b. 0   e. 10

        c. 7

3.025   A solution with a pH of 11 has a [H^+] of _____ .

        a. 11   d. 1×10^{-3}

        b. 1×10^{-11} e. 1×10^{11}

        c. 1×10^{3}

3.026   In a solution with a pH of 4, the [OH^-] is _____ .

        a. 1×10^{-10} d. 4

        b. 1×10^{-4} e. 10

        c. 1×10^{-8}

3.027   What is the normality of 0.01 M solution of $HC_2H_3O_2$?
        ($HC_2H_3O_2 \rightleftharpoons H^+ + C_2H_3O_2^-$)

        a. 0.02 N   d. 0.04 N

        b. 0.005 N   e. 0.01 N

        c. 0.03 N

3.028   Sulfuric acid dissolves in water as $H_2SO_4 \rightleftharpoons 2 H^+ + SO_4^{-2}$. Which of the following solutions of H_2SO_4 will conduct the most electricity?

        a. 1.0 M   d. 2.0 N

        b. 1.0 N   e. 2.0 M

        c. 0.5 N

3.029   If $Na_2B_4O_7$ is added to water, the solution would probably test _____ .

        a. acid   d. dilute

        b. neutral   e. negative

        c. basic

3.030   Our body solution tests at a pH of about 6.8. This pH is _____ .

        a. strongly acidic   d. slightly basic

        b. strongly basic   e. neutral

        c. slightly acidic

Complete these statements (each answer, 3 points).

3.031   A solution where the solid is in equilibrium with the dissolved state is said to be

        _____ .

3.032   The variables affecting the rate of dissolving are the a. _____ ,
        b. _____ , c. _____ , and d. _____ .

3.033   Several characteristics of acids include a. _____ b. _____ ,
        c. _____ , and d. _____ .

3.034   A salt is defined as a _____

        _____ .

3.035   The scale used to describe the amount of acidity or basicity is called _____ .

Make the following calculations (each answer, 5 points).

3.036   Determine the g.f.w. for $Ca_3(PO_4)_2$. $(Ca = 40.0, P = 31.0, O = 16.0)$

3.037   Write the K_{eq} for the reaction $CH_4 + 2 O_2 \rightleftharpoons CO_2 + 2 H_2O$.

3.038   Calculate the molarity of solution given the following information: 10 g of NaOH were dissolved in 500 ml of solution. $(Na = 23; O = 16; H = 1)$.

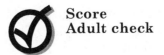

Score _____

Adult check _____

Initial   Date

IV. REDOX EQUILIBRIUMS

Chemical reactions may be divided into two general classes. The first includes reactions in which none of the atoms change their ion charge during the reaction. Examples of this type might include neutralization of acids by bases, formation of precipitates by the combining of ions, and other double replacements. The second class is redox reactions.

Redox Examples:

$$2\ Na_{(g)} + Cl_{2(g)} \longrightarrow 2\ NaCl_{(s)} \text{ (Combination)}$$

$$2\ KClO_{3(s)} \longrightarrow 2\ KCl_{(s)} + 3\ O_{2(g)} \text{ (Decomposition)}$$

$$CaI_{2(s)} + Cl_{2(g)} \longrightarrow CaCl_{2(s)} + I_{2(s)} \text{ (Replacement)}$$

The reaction studied previously involving the copper and silver nitrate was a redox reaction. The net ionic equation could be written:

$$Cu^0_{(s)} + 2\ Ag^+_{(aq)} \longrightarrow Cu^{+2}_{(aq)} + 2\ Ag^0_{(s)}$$

Notice the change in ion charge of both the copper and silver.

Redox reactions are very common in our daily lives. The rusting of iron, the browning of an apple or banana, and the decaying of a log in a forest are examples of redox reactions. The natural decay of our universe is to a great extent the result of oxidation-reduction reactions.

In this section you will study redox reactions, will balance redox equations, and will examine a couple of common examples of oxidation-reduction.

SECTION OBJECTIVES

Review these objectives. When you have completed this section, you should be able to:

16. Identify anions and cations.
17. Identify oxidizing and reducing agents.
18. Write half-reactions.
19. Balance redox reactions.

OXIDATION-REDUCTION

A typical oxidation-reduction reaction can be represented in symbol form:

$$Zn_{(s)} + Cu^{+2} + SO_4^{-2} \rightleftharpoons Zn^{+2} + Cu_{(s)} + SO_4^{-2}$$

What is the net ionic equation?

$$(Zn + Cu^{+2} \rightleftharpoons Zn^{+2} + Cu)$$

Oxidation. Any change in ion charge depends upon the transfer of electrons. For example, sodium is readily changed to form positive sodium ions.

$$Na \longrightarrow Na^+ + e^-$$

We can generalize this equation for any metal by writing: $M \longrightarrow M^+ + Ne^-$, where N represents the number of electrons lost by each metal atom. This type of electron change is called *oxidation*. In an *oxidation system* the atoms show an algebraic increase in ion charge (becomes more positive). *Oxidation* causes a loss of electrons.

Look closely at the Zn as a reactant and then as a product. It follows a reaction which can be represented as $Zn^0_{(s)} \longrightarrow Zn^{+2} + 2e^-$. For the zinc atom to take on a +2 charge, two electrons must have been removed.

Reduction. The opposite process of electron transfer is called *reduction*. Some examples of reduction are shown by the following reactions:

$$S + 2 e^- \longrightarrow S^{-2} \qquad 2 H^+ + 2 e^- \longrightarrow H_2$$

A *reduction system* requires that atoms show an algebraic decrease in ion charge. This is a result of a gain of electrons.

Look closely at the $Cu^{+2} \longrightarrow Cu_{(s)}$ reaction. For this charge to occur, two electrons must have been added to the Cu^{+2} ion: $Cu^{+2} + 2 e^- \longrightarrow Cu^0_{(s)}$.

 Complete this activity.

4.1   Consider the $Zn_{(s)} + Cu^{+2} \rightleftharpoons Zn^{+2} + Cu_{(s)}$ system.

   a. Where did the electrons come from in the system? _____

   b. Which element was the electron donor? _____

   c. Which element was the electron acceptor? _____

   d. Which element must be more willing to give up electrons? _____

Electrochemical cells. Look at the Zn - Cu^{+2} system as a whole.

$$Zn^0_{(s)} \longrightarrow Zn^{+2} + 2 e^- \text{ (oxidation)}$$
$$Cu^{+2} + 2 e^- \longrightarrow Cu^0_{(s)} \text{ (reduction)}$$

$$\overline{Zn^0_{(s)} + Cu^{+2} \longrightarrow Zn^{+2} + Cu_{(s)}}$$

Note: When the two equations are added together, the 2 e⁻'s cancel since they are found on each side of the equation.

In any oxidation-reduction (redox) reaction, the same number of electrons must be donated as are accepted. The tendency of the electrons to be given from one element to another can be measured electrically as well as with the ∆H value. One approach is to measure the electrical force between two different elements. The following experiment was carried out by a chemistry student. If you have the necessary materials, you can reproduce the investigation.

Prepare 2.5 x 1 cm samples of the metals Zn, Cu, and Pb by cleaning them with steel wool. Get the dropper bottles of 1 M solution of soluble salts of each metal, such as, $ZnSO_4$, $CuSO_4$, $Pb(NO_3)_2$, and $NaNO_3$. Notch a 12.5 cm filter paper as shown in Figure 3 and lay it on a 15 cm square glass plate. Place the piece of copper on the moistened paper. Repeat the procedure for $ZnSO_4$ and Zn, and $Pb(NO_3)_2$ and Pb in the remaining sections. Add a drop or two of $NaNO_3$ to the central area to act as a salt bridge between the metal-metal ion sections. Set the vacuum tube voltmeter on the 1.5 volt scale. Check the voltages between pairs of the metals with VTVM and record the readings. The probe connection is the negative electrode and placed on the most active metal when the meter setting is on DC-.

Note: The Al electrode combinations have been determined for you because Al potentials are difficult to measure experimentally with any accuracy.

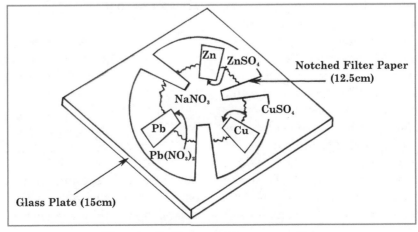

FIGURE 3: ELECTROCHEMICAL CELL

53

The following table was made from the results and observations.

DATA TABLE 11

Cell Pair	Electron Donor (oxidation-anode)	Electron Acceptor (reduction-cathode)	Meter Reading (volts)
Al - Pb	Al	Pb	1.42
Al - Zn	Al	Zn	0.81
Al - Cu	Al	Cu	1.74
Pb - Zn	Zn	Pb	0.55
Pb - Cu	Pb	Cu	0.42
Zn - Cu	Zn	Cu	1.12

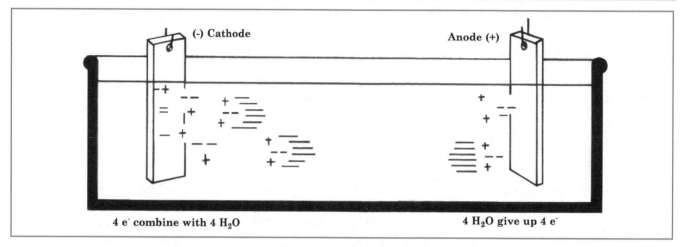

FIGURE 4: ELECTROCHEMICAL CELL

Take a close look at what happens in an *electrochemical* cell (Figure 4). The term electrochemical implies that we are converting chemical energy into electrical energy. Look again at the $Zn - Cu^{+2}$ system. At the zinc electrode, electrons are released and oxidation occurs. The electrode where oxidation occurs is called the *anode*. Electrons are gained at the copper electrode and reduction occurs. The electrode where reduction occurs is called the *cathode*. As electrons leave the cell from the anode, positively charged Zn^{+2} ions are produced. Negative charge is leaving and positive charge is produced. Electrical neutrality is maintained. Because negative ions always drift toward the anode, they are called *anions*. Since positive ions drift away from the anode toward the cathode, they are called *cations*. The Zn^{+2} ion drifts away into solution but electrons remain in the zinc electrode. They move up the zinc electrode, through the wire, and enter the copper cathode. At the surface of the rod, the electrons encounter Cu^{+2} ions in solution. The electrons react with the Cu^{+2} to give neutral copper atoms, which remain on the rod as copper metal. To write separate "half-reaction" equations for the two separate processes is often convenient:

(1) $Zn^0 \longrightarrow Zn^{+2} + 2 e^-$ (oxidation);
(2) $Cu^{+2} + 2 e^- \longrightarrow Cu^0$ (reduction). The net reaction (3) is found by adding the two half-reactants.

$$
\begin{array}{ll}
(1) & Zn^0 \longrightarrow Zn^{+2} + 2 e^- \\
(2) & Cu^{+2} + 2 e^- \longrightarrow Cu^0 \\
\hline
(1) + (2) = (3) & Zn^0 + Cu^{+2} \longrightarrow Zn^{+2} + Cu^0
\end{array}
$$

Notice that the electrons on each side of the equation cancel. If they do not cancel in the half-reactions, as in the $Cu^0 - Ag^+$ reaction, we must first balance the electrons and then add the half-reactions. That is,

$$
\begin{array}{l}
Cu^0 \longrightarrow Cu^{+2} + 2 e^- \\
Ag^+ + e^- \longrightarrow Ag^0 \\
\hline
\text{(INCORRECT)}
\end{array}
$$

$$
\begin{array}{l}
Cu^0 \longrightarrow Cu^{+2} + 2 e^- \\
2Ag^+ + 2e^- \longrightarrow 2Ag^0 \\
\hline
\text{(CORRECT)}
\end{array}
$$

Later in the section you will learn how the balancing of electrons will enable you to write balanced equations for more difficult reactions.

54

Do this activity.

4.2 From your observed cell voltage readings, *attempt* to list these elements: (Zn, Cu, Al, and Pb) in order of decreasing activity. Assume aluminum is the most willing to donate electrons.

Best electron donor = aluminum

a. Second best donor = _____

b. Third best donor = _____

c. Poorest electron donor = _____

To have a table in which the reactants are arranged in the order of their tendency to undergo oxidation (or reduction) is convenient so that we can predict whether a reaction will actually occur if the two substances are placed together. Such a table is known as an oxidation-reduction potential series. It consists of a series of half-reactions written so that the reaction to the right is an oxidation and the reaction to the left is a reduction. A reaction occurs spontaneously if the oxidation half-reaction is higher on the series than the reduction half-reaction.

Since we are comparing half-reactions, it is necessary to have a reference. Therefore, chemists have assigned the half-reaction $H_{2(g)} \longrightarrow 2 H^+ + 2e^-$, an E^0 value of 0.00 volts. All other half-reactions are then measured against the standard hydrogen half-reaction.

Complete these activities.

4.3 Refer to Data Table 12 of oxidation potentials and list the $E^°$ for the following half-reactions:

a. $Zn^0 \rightleftharpoons Zn^{+2} + 2 e^-$ E^0 = _____

b. $Cu^0 \rightleftharpoons Cu^{+2} + 2 e^-$ E^0 = _____

c. $Pb^0 \rightleftharpoons Pb^{+2} + 2 e^-$ E^0 = _____

d. $Al^0 \rightleftharpoons Al^{+3} + 3 e^-$ E^0 = _____

4.4 From these E^0 values in 4.3, list the elements in order of decreasing activity.

a. _____   c. _____

b. _____   d. _____

e. Does this list agree with your previous predictions in 4.2? _____

- -

4.5 *OPTIONAL:* You will find that a knowledge of oxidation-reduction reactions will be a valuable tool as you further your study of chemistry. We have calculated the molar heat of reaction (ΔH). We have found that ΔH is related to the electrode potential (measured voltage for Zn^0 - Cu^{+2} cell) by the following formula:

$\Delta H = -nFE$ Where E = electrode potential (cell voltage from Data Table 11)

n = number of electrons transferred

F = Faraday's Constant = -23,060 cal/volt

Calculated ΔH = For the Zn - Cu^{+2} system

- -

4.6 *OPTIONAL:* The formula in 4.5 gives a simple method of calculating ΔH's if we had values of electrode potentials available. Another relationship exists between the electrode potential and the equilibrium constant: $E = {}^{.059}/_n \log K_{eq}$. Solve this equation for the equilibrium constant and use your observed E to calculate the K_{eq} calculations for the Cu^{+2} - Zn system.

DATA TABLE 12

STANDARD OXIDATION POTENTIALS FOR HALF-REACTIONS
IONIC CONCENTRATIONS, 1 M IN WATER AT 25°

All ions are equated

	Half Reaction	E° (volts)	
Very strong reducing agents	$Li \longrightarrow e^- + Li^+$	3.00	Very weak oxidizing agents
	$Rb \longrightarrow e^- + Rb^+$	2.92	
	$K \longrightarrow e^- + K^+$	2.92	
	$Cs \longrightarrow e^- + Cs^+$	2.92	
	$Ba \longrightarrow 2\,e^- + Ba^{2+}$	2.90	
	$Sr \longrightarrow 2\,e^- + Sr^{2+}$	2.89	
	$Ca \longrightarrow 2\,e^- + Ca^{2+}$	2.87	
	$Na \longrightarrow e^- + Na^+$	2.71	
	$Mg \longrightarrow 2e^- + Mg^{2+}$	2.37	
	$Al \longrightarrow 3\,e^- + Al^{3+}$	1.66	
	$Mn \longrightarrow 2\,e^- + Mn^{2+}$	1.18	
	$H_{2(g)} + 2\,OH^- \longrightarrow 2\,e^- + 2\,H_2O$	0.83	
	$Zn \longrightarrow 2\,e^- + Zn^{2+}$	0.76	
	$Cr \longrightarrow 3\,e^- + Cr^{3+}$	0.74	
	$2\,Ag + S^{2-} \longrightarrow 2\,e^- + Ag_2S$	0.69	
	$Fe \longrightarrow 2\,e^- + Fe^{2+}$	0.44	
	$H_{2(g)} \longrightarrow 2\,e^- + 2\,H^+ \ (10^{-7}\,M)$	0.414	
	$Cr^{2+} \longrightarrow e^- + Cr^{3+}$	0.41	
	$Co \longrightarrow 2\,e^- + Co^{2+}$	0.28	
	$Ni \longrightarrow 2\,e^- + Ni^{2+}$	0.25	
	$Sn \longrightarrow 2\,e^- + Sn^{2+}$	0.14	
	$Pb \longrightarrow 2\,e^- + Pb^{2+}$	0.13	
	$H_{2(g)} \longrightarrow 2\,e^- + 2\,H^+$	0.00	
	$H_2S_{(g)} \longrightarrow 2\,e^- + {}^{1}/_{8}\,S_8 + 2\,H^+$	- 0.14	
	$Sn^{2+} \longrightarrow 2\,e^- + Sn^{4+}$	- 0.15	
	$Cu^+ \longrightarrow e^- + Cu^{2+}$	- 0.15	
	$SO_2(g) + 2\,H_2O \longrightarrow 2\,e^- + SO_4^{2-} + 4\,H^+$	- 0.17	
	$Cu \longrightarrow 2\,e^- + Cu^{2+}$	- 0.34	
	$Cu \longrightarrow e^- + Cu^+$	- 0.52	
	$2\,I^- \longrightarrow 2\,e^- + I_2$	- 0.53	
	$H_2O_v \longrightarrow 2\,e^- + O_{2(g)} + 2\,H^+$	- 0.68	
	$Fe^{2+} \longrightarrow e^- + Fe^{3+}$	- 0.77	
	$NO_2(g) + H_2O \longrightarrow e^- + NO^{3-} + 2\,H^+$	- 0.78	
	$Hg(l) \longrightarrow 2\,e^- + Hg^{2+}$	- 0.78	
	$Hg(l) \longrightarrow e^- + {}^{1}/_{2}\,Hg^{2+}$	- 0.79	
	$Ag \longrightarrow e^- + Ag^+$	- 0.80	
	$H_2O \longrightarrow 2\,e^- + {}^{1}/_{2}\,O_2(g) + 2\,H^+ \ (10^{-7}\,M)$	- 0.815	
	$NO(g) + 2\,H_2O \longrightarrow 3\,e^- + NO_3^- + 4\,H^+$	- 0.96	
	$2\,Br^- \longrightarrow 2\,e^- + Br_2(l)$	- 1.06	
	$H_2O \longrightarrow 2\,e^- + {}^{1}/_{2}\,O_2(g) + 2\,H^+$	- 1.23	
	$Mn^{2+} + 2\,H_2O \longrightarrow 2\,e^- + MnO_2 + 4\,H^+$	- 1.28	
	$2\,Cr^{3+} + 7\,H_2O \longrightarrow 6\,e^- + Cr_2O_7^{2-} + 14\,H^+$	- 1.33	
Very weak reducing agents	$2\,Cl^- \longrightarrow 2\,e^- + Cl_2(g)$	- 1.36	Very strong oxidizing agents
	$Au \longrightarrow 3\,e^- + Au^{3+}$	- 1.50	
	$Mn^{2+} + 4\,H_2O \longrightarrow 5\,e^- + MnO_4^- + 8\,H^+$	- 1.52	
	$2\,H_2O \longrightarrow 2\,e^- + H_2O_2 + 2\,H^+$	- 1.77	
	$2\,F^- \longrightarrow 2\,e^- + F_2(g)$	- 2.87	

Reducing strength increases →

Oxidizing strength increases →

Referring to the half-reaction pairs measured in Data Table 12, the half-reactions (one as the oxidation, one as the reduction) and the equations for the net reactions can be determined. Be sure to balance electrons. List the E^0 value at the end of the half-reaction. When you reverse the half-reaction as written, you reverse the sign of the E^0 value listed. For example, let us consider a Cu^0 - Ag^+ cell. The half-reaction would be:

$$Cu^0 \longrightarrow Cu^{+2} + 2\ e^- \qquad E^0 = -.34 \text{ volts}$$
$$Ag^0 \longrightarrow Ag^{+1} + e^- \qquad E^0 = -.80 \text{ volts}$$

Balance the electrons. (This does not affect E^0.)

$E_3 = E_1 + E_2$

E_1	$Cu^0 \rightleftharpoons Cu^{+2} + 2\ e^-$	$E^0 = -.34$ volts
E_2	$2\ Ag^{+1} + 2\ e^- \rightleftharpoons 2\ Ag^0$	$E^0 = +.80$ volts
E_3	$Cu^0 + 2\ Ag^+ \rightleftharpoons Cu^{+2} + 2\ Ag^0$	E^0 cell $= +.46$ volts

The sign (+ or -) implies the direction the reaction proceeds. A positive value indicates the reaction will proceed as written in the equation.

Complete these activities.

4.7   Calculate the value for the metal pairs tested in Data Table 12. *Show your work.*

a. Al - Pb

b. Al - Zn

c. Al - Cu

d. Pb - Zn

e. Pb - Cu

f. Zn - Cu

4.8   Compare the experimental E values in Data Table 11 with the accepted values calculated in 4.7. Propose some reasons why these two values may be different.

_____

_____

_____

_____

4.9   Using E^0 values determine which of the following reactions are electrically possible. Show your work.

a. $2\ FeCl_3 \longrightarrow 2\ FeCl_2 + Cl_2$ (Fe^{+3} changes to Fe^{+2}; Cl^- changes to Cl)

b. $Mg + Br_2 \longrightarrow MgBr_2$

c. $Cu + H_2O \longrightarrow CuO + H_2$ (Cu changes to Cu^{+2}; H^+ changes to H)

d. $F_2 + Zn \longrightarrow ZnF_2$

e. $Mg(NO_3)_2 + 2\ Ag \longrightarrow 2\ AgNO_3 + Mg$ (Mg^{+2} changes to Mg; Ag changes to Ag^+)

  Adult Check   _____
                                     Initial   Date

58

Oxidation numbers. We are now ready to turn our attention away from oxidation potentials and to take a look at the bookkeeping of electrochemical reactions. *Oxidation numbers* are arbitrary numbers assigned to an atom within a molecule. These numbers are useful in balancing complex equations.

Just as rules are needed in bookkeeping for procedures to follow, a chemist needs a few rules to assist him in his accounting of electron charge. The following rules will assist you in assigning oxidation numbers to various atoms.

1. *The oxidation number of a monatomic ion is equal to the charge on the ion.*
   For example, Na^+ (Group 1), Mg^{+2} (Group 2), and so on.
2. *The oxidation number of any substance in its atomic state is zero.*
3. *The oxidation number of hydrogen in a compound is +1.*
4. *The oxidation number of oxygen in a compound is -2 (except in O_2, O_3, and in peroxides).*
5. *Other oxidation numbers are assigned so that the sum of charges is zero.*
6. *The Laws of Conservation of Charge and Atoms must be followed.*
7. *The halogens (F, Cl, Br, I) are assigned an oxidation number of -1.*

Example: K_3PO_4 K = +1   (Rule 1) $3 K^{+1} = +3$ Therefore,

$O = -2$ (Rule 4) $\underline{4 O^{-2} = -8}$ P = +5   (Rule 6)

Difference = -5

 Complete these activities.

4.10   Test your understanding by assigning oxidation numbers to each element in these compounds. Write the oxidation number for each atom.

a. N_2O _____

b. H_2SO_4 _____

c. KCl _____

d. CO _____

e. NO _____

f. MnO_2 _____

g. N_2O_5 _____

h. $KMnO_4$ _____

i. CO_2 _____

j. N_2O_4 _____

k. $C_{(diamond)}$ _____

We can apply oxidation numbers to balancing equations. For example, in the following equation we can assign oxidation numbers:

$$\begin{array}{cccc} +1\ -2 & 0 & +4\ -2 & +1\ -2 \\ H_2S\ + & O_2 \longrightarrow & SO_2\ + & H_2O \end{array}$$

We see that S^{-2} goes to S^{+4} (oxidation) and that O^0_2 goes to $2\ O^{-2}$ (reduction). Four electrons are involved in the oxidation and four electrons in reduction. The half-reactions for the oxidation and reduction can be written:

oxidation: $S^{-2} \longrightarrow S^{+4} + 6\ e^-$

reduction: $\overline{O_2^0 + 4\ e^- \longrightarrow 2\ O^{-2}}$

The oxidizing agent is the compound that accepts electrons. A reducing agent is any compound or ion that donates electrons.

The electrons are balanced and the half-reactions are rewritten showing the proper mole ratios:

oxidation:

$2\ (S^{-2} \longrightarrow S^{+4} + 6\ e^-) = 2\ S^{-2} \longrightarrow 2\ S^{+4} + 12\ e^-$

reduction:

$3\ (O_2 + 4\ e^- \longrightarrow 2\ O^{-2}) = 3\ O_2 + 12\ e^- \longrightarrow 6\ O^-$

The final step is to transfer these mole ratios to the original equation and to make any necessary adjustments in order to conserve the atoms.

The completed balanced equation is written:

$$2 H_2S + 3 O_2 \longrightarrow 2 SO_2 + 2H_2O$$

 Complete these activities.

4.11   Balance the following redox equations by the use of oxidation numbers.

a. $KMnO_4 + H_2S + HCl \rightleftharpoons KCl + MnCl_2 + H_2O + S$

oxidizing agent = _____   reducing agent = _____

b. $HBr + H_2SO_4 \rightleftharpoons SO_2 + Br_2 + H_2O$

oxidizing agent = _____   reducing agent = _____

c. $Cu + HNO_3 \rightleftharpoons Cu(NO_3)_2 + H_2O + NO$

oxidizing agent = _____   reducing agent = _____

d. $AlCl_3 + Na \rightleftharpoons NaCl + Al$

oxidizing agent = _____   reducing agent = _____

 Adult Check _____
                          Initial   Date

4.12   *OPTIONAL:* What is the E^0 for cobalt? _____ What is the E^0 for hydrogen? _____
On the basis of these E^0 values, will cobalt metal dissolve in a 1M solution of acid, H^+?
_____ Attach your answer.

4.13   *OPTIONAL:* Write a completed balanced equation for this reaction. Attach your work.

$$FeSO_4 + KMnO_4 + H_2SO_4 \longrightarrow MnSO_4 + H_2O + Fe_2(SO_4)_3 + K_2SO_4$$

4.14   *OPTIONAL:* Write a complete balanced equation for this reaction. Use half-reactions. Attach your work.

$$Pb_3H_4IO_6 + HCl + H_3AsO_3 \longrightarrow PbCl_2 + ICl + H_3AsO_4 + H_2O$$

Adult Check   _____
                Initial   Date

APPLICATION

The browning of fruit when exposed to air, the tarnishing of silver, and the rusting of iron are all examples of redox reactions. In this section you will study just a few of the applications of redox chemistry.

Complete this investigation.

> **These supplies are needed:**
> shiny silver (coin, tableware)
> source of sulfur (powdered sulfur, egg yolk, strike anywhere match)

Follow these steps and complete the activities. Put a check in the box when each step is completed.

❏ 1. Place the silver and sulfur in contact with each other for at least twenty minutes.

❏ 2. Clean the silver gently.

❏ 3. Observe and record what you see in 4.15.

4.15   Record your observations. _____
_____

4.16   Balance the equation for the reaction. _____

Complete this investigation.

> **These supplies are needed:**
> heat source
> aluminum pan
> baking soda ($NaHCO_3$)
> tarnished silver (from above or others that are available)
> water for rinsing

Follow these directions and complete the activities. Put a check in the box when each step is completed.

❏ 1. Add two or three heaping teaspoons of $NaHCO_3$ for each quart of water in the aluminum pan.

❏ 2. Stir the $NaHCO_3$ into the water.

❏ 3. Heat the pan and solution.

❏ 4. When the solution is hot, hold the tarnished silver in the solution. Have the silver touch the aluminum. Some bubbling will take place in the solution. Some carbon dioxide gas is liberated and the solution becomes alkaline. Alkaline solutions react chemically with aluminum. Under these conditions the tarnish on the silver is changed back to silver, a chemical change.

❏ 5. Rinse the silver article with fresh water and dry it. (Later a complete immersion will clean the entire piece of silver.)

4.17   Using the half-reactions, balance the equation for the Ag - Al system and determine the E value for the reaction.

 Do this investigation.

> **These supplies are needed:**
> fresh apple
> seven test tubes with stoppers (small container like baby food jars with lids)
> boiled water
> tap water
> ascorbic acid (Vitamin C) tablets
> juice known to contain Vitamin C

 Follow these directions and do the activities. Put a check in the box when each step is completed.

❏ 1. Line up the seven containers and label from 1 to 7.

❏ 2. Tube 1: Apple slice open to air — no liquid.

❏ 3. Tube 2: Apple slice and the tube closed so that a limited supply of oxygen is available — no liquid.

❏ 4. Tube 3: Cover the slice with tap water.

❏ 5. Tube 4: Cover the slice and fill the tube with water that has been boiled to rid it of most of the dissolved oxygen. Close this tube with as little air as possible above the water.

Notice that a decreasing amount of oxygen is available in Tubes 1 through 4.

❑ 6. Tube 5: Cover the slice with ascorbic acid solution (with lemon juice or with solution of a crushed Vitamin C tablet).

❑ 7. Tube 6: Cover the slice with another concentration of the solution used in Tube 5.

❑ 8. Tube 7 and others: Cover the slice with equal volumes of known sources of Vitamin C such as orange juice (canned, fresh, frozen), grapefruit juice, papaya juice, green-pepper juice, tomato juice, or canned beverage which is marked on the label as "Vitamin C added."

❑ 9. Let tubes stand undisturbed until the second day.

❑ 10. Use the discoloration rate of the contents of Tube 1 as a standard. Compare all the others with Tube 1, as well as with each other. Make a written tabulation in 4.18 by rating the discoloration. Give the Tube 1 a value of 10.

4.18 Record of observations.

Tube	Rated Discoloration	Observations
1	10	
2		
3		
4		
5		
6		
7		

Adult Check _____
　　　　　　　Initial　　　Date

4.19 Is the presence of oxygen a factor in discoloring of fresh fruit? _____

4.20 Ascorbic acid is a mild reducing agent. Could another mild reducing agent be used to retard darkening, a dilute solution of sulfur dioxide, for example, or benzaldehyde?

_____

_____

_____

4.21 Is any difference noted between Vitamin C from natural sources and Vitamin C made synthetically? _____

_____

_____

Adult Check _____
　　　　　　　Initial　　　Date

4.22   *OPTIONAL:* Tomato juice is known to be acidic. Why is it never wise to heat tomato juice in an aluminum pan? Explain in depth on an attached paper.

4.23   *OPTIONAL:* A patient went to her dentist and said that every time she bit down on anything aluminum and it contacted her silver filling, she experienced a painful sensation. How might you explain this experience in terms of an electrochemical reaction? Attach your explanation.

4.24   *OPTIONAL:* Some green or blue material often collects on the posts on top of a car battery. If the green material is scraped off by using an iron screwdriver, the screwdriver becomes copper-coated. Give a possible formula for the green or blue substance and explain where it could have possibly come from. (The liquid in the battery is H_2SO_4 and the connecting cables are copper wires.) Include your answer with the LIFEPAC.

4.25   *OPTIONAL:* Many of us have experienced trying to start a car and finding that the battery was "dead." What has happened chemically to this electrochemical system? What is the K_{eq}? Has equilibrium been reached? How can you tell? Record your answers on attached sheets.

Adult Check _____
                  Initial   Date

Before you finish Section IV and take Self Test 4, some review problems will help to prepare you. Review Section IV carefully before you try these review activities.

Complete these activities.

4.26   What are the oxidation numbers of nitrogen in the following:

a. NO_2 _____   e. NO_3^- _____

b. NO _____   f. N_3O_6 _____

c. N_2O_4 _____   g. N_2O_5 _____

d. NO_3 _____

4.27   Consider this reaction.

a. When M^{+2} undergoes a chemical reaction to produce M^{+6}, has oxidation or reduction occurred?

    _____

b. Write a general mathematical sentence to show this change.

4.28   A copper spoon was accidentally used to stir a solution of 1 M Cr^{+3} ions. What do you expect to happen? Explain your answer using E^0 values.

4.29   Use the reaction:

$5 H_2S_{(g)} + 2 Na^+ + 2MnO_4^- + 6H^+ + 3 SO_4^{-2} \longrightarrow 5 S_{(g)} + 2 Mn^{+2} + 2 Na^+ + 8 H_2O + 3 SO_4^{-2}$

a. Which ions are spectator ions? _____

b. For each 5 moles of H₂S used, how many moles of H₂O are produced? _____

c. For each 5 moles of H₂S used, how many moles of electrons are transferred? _____

d. Write the net ionic equation for the previous reaction.

 Circle the letter of the correct response.

4.30   Consider the reaction of ____ $HI + H_2SO_4 \longrightarrow 4I_2 + H_2S + $ ____ H_2O.

What are the coefficients of HI and H₂O, respectively, necessary to balance this expression?

a. 2 and 1   d. 8 and 4

b. 4 and 4   e. 1 and 2

c. 6 and 3   f. neither a, b, c, d, or e

4.31   When a piece of magnesium is connected to an iron pipe, the iron is prevented from corroding. Which of the following is the best explanation?

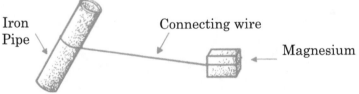

a. Magnesium reacts with the ground water to form a protective coat on the iron pipe of $Mg(OH)_2$.

b. Magnesium atoms replace the iron atoms lost when the iron corrodes.

c. Electrons flow from the iron through the wire to the magnesium leaving a protective coating of Fe^{+3} on the pipe.

d. When magnesium corrodes, electrons flow through the wire to the iron pipe, thus preventing the iron atoms from losing electrons.

e. The electric current flowing through the ground from the magnesium to the iron kills the organisms which attack and corrode the pipe.

 Adult Check _____
                    Initial   Date

Before you take this last Self Test, you may want to do one or more of these self checks.

1. _____ Read the objectives. Determine if you can do them.

2. _____ Restudy the material related to any objectives that you cannot do.

3. _____ Use the SQ3R study procedure to review the material:
   a. **S**can the sections.
   b. **Q**uestion yourself again (review the questions you wrote initially).
   c. **R**ead to answer your questions.
   d. **R**ecite the answers to yourself.
   e. **R**eview areas you didn't understand.

4. _____ Review all vocabulary, activities, and Self Tests, writing a correct answer for each wrong answer.

Answer *true* **or** *false* (each answer, 1 point).

4.01 _____ Covalent solutions are good conductors of electricity.

4.02 _____ An acid has OH^- ions in its formula.

4.03 _____ Acids are sour.

4.04 _____ A base has H^+.

4.05 _____ Precipitation occurs when the K_{sp} is exceeded.

Choose the correct answer (each answer, 3 points).

4.06 If a crystal of KNO_3 is added to a *saturated* water solution of KNO_3 at 20°C, it will _____ .

   a. dissolve

   b. cause the KNO_3 to crystallize out

   c. remain apparently unchanged

   d. lower the freezing point of the solution

4.07 The reason for the correct answer in 4.06 is that _____ .

   a. KNO_3 is highly soluble in water

   b. KNO_3 must precipitate since the solution is saturated

   c. the system is already in equilibrium; hence, the rate of solution equals the rate of crystallization. Therefore, no apparent change should occur.

   d. salts lower the freezing point of water

4.08 Which of the following would be expected to form ionic solutions in water?

   a. CO_2 c. C e. NaI

   b. CCl_4 d. O_2

4.09 What is the equilibrium concentration of Ag^+ ions in a saturated aqueous solution of AgCl made by shaking AgCl with water? ($K_{sp} < 1 \times 10^{-10}$)

   a. 1×10^{-20} c. 1×10^{-10} e. 0.5×10^{-5}

   b. 1×10^{-5} d. 2×10^{-10}

4.010 Which of the following pairs of ions would be expected to form precipitates when dilute solutions are mixed? Write the formulas for the precipitates formed. Use Data Table 8 as a reference.

   a. Na^+, SO_4^{-2} c. NH_4^+, CO_3^{-2} e. Pb^{+2}, Cl^- g. Ca^{+2}, PO_4^{-3}

   b. Ba^{+2}, CO_3^{-2} d. Fe^{+3}, OH^- f. Na^+, S^{-2}

4.011 The solubility of strontium sulfate, $SrSO_4$, at room temperature is 8.0×10^{-4} moles per liter. The calculated K_{sp} for $SrSO_4$ is _____ .

   a. 4.0×10^{-4} c. 6.4×10^{-7} e. 6.4×10^{-9}

   b. 8.0×10^{-4} d. 16.0×10^{-8}

4.012 Which of the following statements is true of cations?

   a. Cations are attracted to the anode.

   b. Cations undergo oxidation at the proper electrode.

   c. Cations undergo reduction at the proper electrode.

   d. Cations are negatively charged.

4.013   Electrolytes are defined as those compounds which _____ .

    a. have covalent bonding

    b. produce less lowering at the freezing point than do compounds like sugar

    c. have only ionic bonds

    d. dissolve in a solvent such as water to produce a solution which conducts electric current easily

4.014   Select the compound in which chlorine is assigned the oxidation number +5.

    a. $HClO_4$ c. $HClO_2$ e. HCl

    b. $NaClO_3$ d. HClO

4.015   The reaction $2\ Cu\ +\ O_2\ \longrightarrow\ 2\ CuO$ has long been called an oxidation-reaction. Copper also reacts with chlorine: $Cu\ +\ Cl_2\ \longrightarrow\ CuCl_2$. In such a reaction _____ .

    a. copper is also oxidized even though no oxygen is present

    b. chlorine is oxidized

    c. oxidation occurs but reduction does not

    d. there is no change in oxidation numbers

4.016   The K_{sp} expression for the system $PbCl_{2(s)}\ \rightleftharpoons\ Pb^{+2}_{(aq)}\ +\ 2Cl^-_{(aq)}$ is _____ .

    a. $[PbCl_2]\ [Pb^{+2}]\ [2Cl^-]$ c. $[Pb^{+2}]\ [Cl^-]^2$ e. $\dfrac{[Pb^+][Cl^-]^2}{[PbCl_2]}$

    b. $[PbCl_2]\ [Pb^{+2}]\ [Cl^-]^2$ d. $[Pb^{+2}]\ [2\ Cl^-]^2\ [PbCl^-]^2$

4.017   Which of the following diagrams best describes the enthalpy of a spontaneous precipitation reaction like $Ag^+\ +\ Cl^-\ \rightleftharpoons\ AgCl$?

a.   b.   c.   d.

Complete these statements (each answer, 3 points).

4.018   The g.f.w. of H_2SO_4 is _____ .

    (H = 1; S = 32; O = 16)

4.019   The characteristics of an acid are a. _____ ,

    b. _____ , c. _____ , and d. _____ .

4.020   A salt is defined as _____

_____

4.021   The conductivity of a solution depends upon a. _____ ,

    b. _____ , c. _____ , and d. _____ .

4.022   A solution conducts electricity because the solution contains _____ .

4.023   Assuming equal number of potential ions, as ionic character increases, the conductivity

_____ .

4.024   In the compound $K_2Cr_2O_7$ the Cr has an oxidation number of _____ .

4.025   The scale used to describe acidity or basicity is called _____ .

Make the following calculations (each answer, 5 points).

4.026   Determine the number of grams of NaCl necessary to make up 100 ml of a 0.1 M solution.
(Na = 23.0; Cl = 35.5)

4.027   Determine the net voltage for the following electrochemical cell: $Zn - Cu^{+2}$.

4.028   The pH of an acetic acid solution is 4.0.

a. Calculate the $[H^+]$.

b. What is the pOH?

4.029   The solubility of BaC_2O_4 in water is 0.093 g/liter. If the g.f.w. = 225 and the substance dissolves
as $BaC_2O_4 \rightleftharpoons Ba^{+2} + C_2O_4 \rightleftharpoons Ba^{+2} + C_2O_4^{-2}$, determine the K_{sp}. O_4^{-2}, determine the K_{sp}.

SHOW YOUR WORK.

86
/108

Before taking the LIFEPAC Test, you may want to do one or more of these self checks.

1. _____ Read the objectives. Check to see if you can do them.

2. _____ Restudy the material related to any objectives that you cannot do.

3. _____ Use the SQ3R study procedure to review the material.

4. _____ Review activities Self Tests, and LIFEPAC vocabulary words.

5. _____ Restudy areas of weakness indicated by the last Self Test.

PERIODIC TABLE
Atomic Properties of the Elements

NIST
National Institute of
Standards and Technology
U.S. Department of Commerce

Physical Measurement Laboratory
www.nist.gov/pml

Standard Reference Data
www.nist.gov/srd

Frequently used fundamental physical constants

For the most accurate values of these and other constants, visit physics.nist.gov/constants
1 second = 9 192 631 770 periods of radiation corresponding to the transition between the two hyperfine levels of the ground state of ^{133}Cs

speed of light in vacuum	c	299 792 458 m s^{-1} (exact)
Planck constant	h	6.626 07 × 10^{-34} J s ($\hbar = h/2\pi$)
elementary charge	e	1.602 177 × 10^{-19} C
electron mass	m_e	9.109 38 × 10^{-31} kg
	$m_e c^2$	0.510 999 MeV
proton mass	m_p	1.672 622 × 10^{-27} kg
fine-structure constant	α	1/137.035 999
Rydberg constant	R_∞	10 973 731.569 m^{-1}
	$R_\infty c$	3.289 841 960 × 10^{15} Hz
	$R_\infty hc$	13.605 69 eV
Boltzmann constant	k	1.380 6 × 10^{-23} J K^{-1}

Legend: Solids, Liquids, Gases, Artificially Prepared

Key (example):
58 — Atomic Number
Ce — Symbol
Cerium — Name
140.116 — Standard Atomic Weight†
[Xe]4f5d6s² — Ground-state Configuration
$^1G^\circ_4$ — Ground-state Level
5.5386 — Ionization Energy (eV)

Group / Period elements

Group 1 (IA)
1 H Hydrogen 1.008* 1s $^2S_{1/2}$ 13.5984
3 Li Lithium 6.94* 1s²2s 5.3917 $^2S_{1/2}$
11 Na Sodium 22.98976928 [Ne]3s 5.1391 $^2S_{1/2}$
19 K Potassium 39.0983 [Ar]4s 4.3407 $^2S_{1/2}$
37 Rb Rubidium 85.4678 [Kr]5s 4.1771 $^2S_{1/2}$
55 Cs Cesium 132.9054519 [Xe]6s 3.8939 $^2S_{1/2}$
87 Fr Francium (223) [Rn]7s 4.0727 $^2S_{1/2}$

Group 2 (IIA)
4 Be Beryllium 9.012182 1s²2s² 9.3227 $^1S_0$
12 Mg Magnesium 24.3050 [Ne]3s² 7.6462 $^1S_0$
20 Ca Calcium 40.078 [Ar]4s² 6.1132 $^1S_0$
38 Sr Strontium 87.62 [Kr]5s² 5.6949 $^1S_0$
56 Ba Barium 137.327 [Xe]6s² 5.2117 $^1S_0$
88 Ra Radium (226) [Rn]7s² 5.2784 $^1S_0$

Group 3 (IIIB)
21 Sc Scandium 44.955912 [Ar]3d4s² 6.5615 $^2D_{3/2}$
39 Y Yttrium 88.90585 [Kr]4d5s² 6.2173 $^2D_{3/2}$

Group 4 (IVB)
22 Ti Titanium 47.867 [Ar]3d²4s² 6.8281 $^3F_2$
40 Zr Zirconium 91.224 [Kr]4d²5s² 6.6339 $^3F_2$
72 Hf Hafnium 178.49 [Xe]4f¹⁴5d²6s² 6.8251 $^3F_2$
104 Rf Rutherfordium (265) [Rn]5f¹⁴6d²7s² 6.01 $^3F_2$

Group 5 (VB)
23 V Vanadium 50.9415 [Ar]3d³4s² 6.7462 $^4F_{3/2}$
41 Nb Niobium 92.90638 [Kr]4d⁴5s 6.7589 $^6D_{1/2}$
73 Ta Tantalum 180.94788 [Xe]4f¹⁴5d³6s² 7.5496 $^4F_{3/2}$
105 Db Dubnium (268) [Rn]5f¹⁴6d³7s² 6.8 $^4F_{3/2}$

Group 6 (VIB)
24 Cr Chromium 51.9961 [Ar]3d⁵4s 6.7665 $^7S_3$
42 Mo Molybdenum 95.96 [Kr]4d⁵5s 7.0924 $^7S_3$
74 W Tungsten 183.84 [Xe]4f¹⁴5d⁴6s² 7.8640 $^5D_0$
106 Sg Seaborgium (271) [Rn]5f¹⁴6d⁴7s² 7.8 $^5D_0$

Group 7 (VIIB)
25 Mn Manganese 54.938045 [Ar]3d⁵4s² 7.4340 $^6S_{5/2}$
43 Tc Technetium (98) [Kr]4d⁵5s² 7.1194 $^6S_{5/2}$
75 Re Rhenium 186.207 [Xe]4f¹⁴5d⁵6s² 7.8335 $^6S_{5/2}$
107 Bh Bohrium (270) [Rn]5f¹⁴6d⁵7s² 7.7 $^6S_{5/2}$

Group 8 (VIII)
26 Fe Iron 55.845 [Ar]3d⁶4s² 7.9025 $^5D_4$
44 Ru Ruthenium 101.07 [Kr]4d⁷5s 7.3605 $^5F_5$
76 Os Osmium 190.23 [Xe]4f¹⁴5d⁶6s² 8.4382 $^5D_4$
108 Hs Hassium (277) [Rn]5f¹⁴6d⁶7s² 7.6 $^5D_4$

Group 9 (VIII)
27 Co Cobalt 58.933195 [Ar]3d⁷4s² 7.8810 $^4F_{9/2}$
45 Rh Rhodium 102.90550 [Kr]4d⁸5s 7.4589 $^4F_{9/2}$
77 Ir Iridium 192.217 [Xe]4f¹⁴5d⁷6s² 8.9670 $^4F_{9/2}$
109 Mt Meitnerium (276)

Group 10 (VIII)
28 Ni Nickel 58.6934 [Ar]3d⁸4s² 7.6399 $^3F_4$
46 Pd Palladium 106.42 [Kr]4d¹⁰ 8.3369 $^1S_0$
78 Pt Platinum 195.084 [Xe]4f¹⁴5d⁹6s 8.9588 $^3D_3$
110 Ds Darmstadtium (281)

Group 11 (IB)
29 Cu Copper 63.546 [Ar]3d¹⁰4s 7.7264 $^2S_{1/2}$
47 Ag Silver 107.8682 [Kr]4d¹⁰5s 7.5762 $^2S_{1/2}$
79 Au Gold 196.966569 [Xe]4f¹⁴5d¹⁰6s 9.2256 $^2S_{1/2}$
111 Rg Roentgenium (280)

Group 12 (IIB)
30 Zn Zinc 65.38 [Ar]3d¹⁰4s² 9.3942 $^1S_0$
48 Cd Cadmium 112.411 [Kr]4d¹⁰5s² 8.9938 $^1S_0$
80 Hg Mercury 200.59 [Xe]4f¹⁴5d¹⁰6s² 10.4375 $^1S_0$
112 Cn Copernicium (285)

Group 13 (IIIA)
5 B Boron 10.81* 1s²2s²2p 8.2980 $^2P^\circ_{1/2}$
13 Al Aluminum 26.9815386 [Ne]3s²3p 5.9858 $^2P^\circ_{1/2}$
31 Ga Gallium 69.723 [Ar]3d¹⁰4s²4p 5.9993 $^2P^\circ_{1/2}$
49 In Indium 114.818 [Kr]4d¹⁰5s²5p 5.7864 $^2P^\circ_{1/2}$
81 Tl Thallium 204.38* [Hg]6p 6.1083 $^2P^\circ_{1/2}$
113 Uut Ununtrium (284)

Group 14 (IVA)
6 C Carbon 12.011* 1s²2s²2p² 11.2603 $^3P_0$
14 Si Silicon 28.085* [Ne]3s²3p² 8.1517 $^3P_0$
32 Ge Germanium 72.63 [Ar]3d¹⁰4s²4p² 7.8994 $^3P_0$
50 Sn Tin 118.710 [Kr]4d¹⁰5s²5p² 7.3439 $^3P_0$
82 Pb Lead 207.2 [Hg]6p² 7.4167 $^3P_0$
114 Fl Flerovium (289)

Group 15 (VA)
7 N Nitrogen 14.007* 1s²2s²2p³ 14.5341 $^4S^\circ_{3/2}$
15 P Phosphorus 30.973762 [Ne]3s²3p³ 10.4867 $^4S^\circ_{3/2}$
33 As Arsenic 74.92160 [Ar]3d¹⁰4s²4p³ 9.7886 $^4S^\circ_{3/2}$
51 Sb Antimony 121.760 [Kr]4d¹⁰5s²5p³ 8.6084 $^4S^\circ_{3/2}$
83 Bi Bismuth 208.98040 [Hg]6p³ 7.2855 $^4S^\circ_{3/2}$
115 Uup Ununpentium (288)

Group 16 (VIA)
8 O Oxygen 15.999* 1s²2s²2p⁴ 13.6181 $^3P_2$
16 S Sulfur 32.06* [Ne]3s²3p⁴ 10.3600 $^3P_2$
34 Se Selenium 78.96 [Ar]3d¹⁰4s²4p⁴ 9.7524 $^3P_2$
52 Te Tellurium 127.60 [Kr]4d¹⁰5s²5p⁴ 9.0097 $^3P_2$
84 Po Polonium (209) [Hg]6p⁴ 8.414 $^3P_2$
116 Lv Livermorium (293)

Group 17 (VIIA)
9 F Fluorine 18.998 4032 1s²2s²2p⁵ 17.4228 $^2P^\circ_{3/2}$
17 Cl Chlorine 35.45* [Ne]3s²3p⁵ 12.9676 $^2P^\circ_{3/2}$
35 Br Bromine 79.904 [Ar]3d¹⁰4s²4p⁵ 11.8138 $^2P^\circ_{3/2}$
53 I Iodine 126.90447 [Kr]4d¹⁰5s²5p⁵ 10.4513 $^2P^\circ_{3/2}$
85 At Astatine (210) [Hg]6p⁵ 9.350 $^2P^\circ_{3/2}$
117 Uus Ununseptium (294)

Group 18 (VIIIA)
2 He Helium 4.002602 1s² 24.5874 $^1S_0$
10 Ne Neon 20.1797 1s²2s²2p⁶ 21.5645 $^1S_0$
18 Ar Argon 39.948 [Ne]3p⁶ 15.7596 $^1S_0$
36 Kr Krypton 83.798 [Ar]3d¹⁰4s²4p⁶ 13.9996 $^1S_0$
54 Xe Xenon 131.293 [Kr]4d¹⁰5s²5p⁶ 12.1298 $^1S_0$
86 Rn Radon (222) [Hg]6p⁶ 10.7485 $^1S_0$
118 Uuo Ununoctium (294)

Lanthanides

57 La Lanthanum 138.90547 [Xe]5d6s² 5.5769 $^2D_{3/2}$
58 Ce Cerium 140.116 [Xe]4f5d6s² 5.5386 $^1G^\circ_4$
59 Pr Praseodymium 140.90765 [Xe]4f³6s² 5.473 $^4I^\circ_{9/2}$
60 Nd Neodymium 144.242 [Xe]4f⁴6s² 5.5250 $^5I_4$
61 Pm Promethium (145) [Xe]4f⁵6s² 5.582 $^6H^\circ_{5/2}$
62 Sm Samarium 150.36 [Xe]4f⁶6s² 5.6437 $^7F_0$
63 Eu Europium 151.964 [Xe]4f⁷6s² 5.6704 $^8S^\circ_{7/2}$
64 Gd Gadolinium 157.25 [Xe]4f⁷5d6s² 6.1498 $^9D^\circ_2$
65 Tb Terbium 158.92535 [Xe]4f⁹6s² 5.8638 $^6H^\circ_{15/2}$
66 Dy Dysprosium 162.500 [Xe]4f¹⁰6s² 5.9391 $^5I_8$
67 Ho Holmium 164.93032 [Xe]4f¹¹6s² 6.0215 $^4I^\circ_{15/2}$
68 Er Erbium 167.259 [Xe]4f¹²6s² 6.1077 $^3H_6$
69 Tm Thulium 168.93421 [Xe]4f¹³6s² 6.1843 $^2F^\circ_{7/2}$
70 Yb Ytterbium 173.054 [Xe]4f¹⁴6s² 6.2542 $^1S_0$
71 Lu Lutetium 174.9668 [Xe]4f¹⁴5d6s² 5.4259 $^2D_{3/2}$

Actinides

89 Ac Actinium (227) [Rn]6d7s² 5.3802 $^2D_{3/2}$
90 Th Thorium 232.03806 [Rn]6d²7s² 6.3067 $^3F_2$
91 Pa Protactinium 231.03588 [Rn]5f²6d7s² 5.89 $^4K_{11/2}$
92 U Uranium 238.02891 [Rn]5f³6d7s² 6.1941 $^5L^\circ_6$
93 Np Neptunium (237) [Rn]5f⁴6d7s² 6.2655 $^6L_{11/2}$
94 Pu Plutonium (244) [Rn]5f⁶7s² 6.0258 $^7F_0$
95 Am Americium (243) [Rn]5f⁷7s² 5.9738 $^8S^\circ_{7/2}$
96 Cm Curium (247) [Rn]5f⁷6d7s² 5.9914 $^9D^\circ_2$
97 Bk Berkelium (247) [Rn]5f⁹7s² 6.1978 $^6H^\circ_{15/2}$
98 Cf Californium (251) [Rn]5f¹⁰7s² 6.2817 $^5I_8$
99 Es Einsteinium (252) [Rn]5f¹¹7s² 6.3676 $^4I^\circ_{15/2}$
100 Fm Fermium (257) [Rn]5f¹²7s² 6.50 $^3H_6$
101 Md Mendelevium (258) [Rn]5f¹³7s² 6.58 $^2F^\circ_{7/2}$
102 No Nobelium (259) [Rn]5f¹⁴7s² 6.65 $^1S_0$
103 Lr Lawrencium (262) [Rn]5f¹⁴7s²7p 4.90 $^2P^\circ_{1/2}$

† Based upon ^{12}C. ( ) indicates the mass number of the longest-lived isotope.

*IUPAC conventional atomic weights; standard atomic weights for these elements are expressed in intervals; see iupac.org for an explanation and values.

For a description of the data, visit physics.nist.gov/data

NIST SP 966 (March 2013)